Dealbreakers and Breakthroughs

The Ten Most Common and Costly Negotiation Mistakes and How to Overcome Them

JOHN ILICH

John Wiley & Sons, Inc.
New York • Chichester • Brisbane • Toronto • Singapore

In recognition of the importance of preserving what
has been written, it is a policy of John Wiley & Sons,
Inc., to have books of enduring value published in
the United States printed on acid-free paper, and we
exert our best efforts to that end.

Library of Congress Cataloging-in-Publication Data:

Ilich, John, 1933–
   Dealbreakers and breakthroughs : the ten most
common and costly negotiation mistakes and
how to overcome them / John Ilich.
     p.   cm.
   Includes bibliographical references.
   ISBN 0-471-53041-7 (acid-free paper)
   1. Negotiation.   I. Title.
BF637.N4I443   1992
158'.5—dc20   90-26721

Printed in the United States of America

10 9 8 7 6 5 4 3 2 1

Printed and bound by Courier Companies, Inc.

Contents

Don't ignore time as a negotiating weapon.
Setting deadlines creates opponent anxiety,
clarifies issues, and can frequently result in
a quick resolution of issues. A deadline,
however, can be a two-edged sword. When
you set one, make sure you know what
you're doing and the consequences that
could result.

If your negotiation seems to have reached an
impasse, don't make the mistake of giving
up. When all else fails, persist and create
fresh approaches with new supporting facts
and insights into the problem causing the
impasse.

One of the cardinal sins of negotiating is
letting your opponent "think things over."
Know the art of closing and the ways to get
your opponent to be a willing accomplice.

Dealbreakers and Breakthroughs

Introduction

E. H. Harriman, the legendary railroad builder and speculator, once remarked to a young financier: "Let me be but one of fifteen men around a table and I will have my way." Bold? Confident? Yes. But more than that, Harriman was superbly schooled in the art of negotiation. He got *what* he wanted because he knew *how* to get what he wanted. And in the final analysis, it is results that count.

Negotiation is one of the most universal forms of human conduct. In the fast-paced, ever-changing, and demanding business and professional world, it prevails. Consider this rather typical headline from *The Detroit News**: "Eastern Deal Falls Through." A proposed $464-million purchase of strike-bound Eastern Airlines collapsed over an impasse in talks between the company's unions and its partner, Texas Air. The key issue blocking an agreement was who would run the airline in an interim period between completion of the deal and the airline's emergence from bankruptcy.

The Eastern Airlines negotiation reflects the high stakes on the table in business today. In fact, business deals commonly involve billions of dollars. Such deals of necessity entail complicated and extensive negotiations with a diverse cast of participants, including the principals themselves, lawyers, accountants, bankers and other lenders, and personal advisors.

Even if these high-stake negotiations resulted in an agreement, the parties may not have gotten all that they wanted. Any or all of those involved may have had to sacrifice a substantial portion of their objectives in order to close the deal. For example, someone may have had to make significant, and unintended, concessions on price, the cost of borrowing the money to fund the deal, or other terms and conditions. Failure to make those concessions, however, would have been a dealbreaker.

---

*April 13, 1989.

A deal is, therefore, not always a *good* deal. Numerous large corporate buyouts, for example, could be described as failures or near failures because the terms negotiated, especially the price paid, were too burdensome to be sustained by the cash flow generated from the transaction. Often, the deal is *bad* because negotiators committed one or more common, but devastating, mistakes discussed in this book. It only takes one mistake to scuttle a negotiation or severely cripple even a consummated agreement. When a deal collapses, chances are that one or more ordinary but potent negotiating mistakes was the culprit.

Deals either succeed or fail primarily because of the negotiating skills of both parties. Whether they involve billions of dollars or no dollars, *all negotiations are contests pitting one mind against another.* In that regard, negotiations are very similar to chess matches, but without the luxury of rules to guide and restrict the players. Negotiations often become wide open, free-wheeling affairs, shaped only by the character and integrity of the negotiators and limited only by their ability and imagination. One side moves; the other assesses and counters. Both sides play to win.

The burden of determining whether a deal is made and whether it is viable, healthy, and beneficial rests squarely on the shoulders of the negotiators. Often when a deal is about to fall through, negotiators will begin to experience a deep depression, which leads to the conclusion that they must make material concessions they had not intended to make in order to save the deal. That feeling leads to fatal errors. Depressed and desperate negotiators might fail to maintain their negotiating bases, to equalize their positions, or to set deadlines for acceptance of proposals. They could improperly use their negotiating power or not even recognize they possessed power that, if timely employed, would make the breakthrough that clinched the deal.

My goal in this book is to help you as a negotiator

make the breakthroughs that define success in negotiations. In each chapter, I focus on one of the ten critical areas of negotiation. I highlight both the potential pitfalls that lead to mistakes and the strategies for avoiding them and achieving your objectives. Chapter 1 tells how to avoid mental rigidity by preparing thoroughly for each negotiating issue. Chapter 2 explains the importance of knowing who has the final negotiating authority. Chapter 3 relates how to use negotiating power at the right time. In Chapter 4, I describe a step-by-step process of setting objectives for each issue. Chapter 5 addresses the problem of equalizing a negotiation. Maintaining control, chiefly through the fine art of funneling, is the concern of Chapter 6. Chapters 7 and 8 deal, respectively, with making offers and counteroffers and with setting deadlines. The value of persistence is the lesson of Chapter 9. Finally, Chapter 10 details the right way to close a negotiation.

Being human, negotiators routinely make errors. Unfortunately, negotiating errors can be both personally and financially devastating. Once mistakes are made, erring negotiators find it difficult to impossible to recover their previous position. It is like spilling a glass of water on an absorbent surface. You can sop up the water and try to put it back in the glass, but you never get it all.

The best way to dodge the dealbreakers is, therefore, to avoid making the negotiating mistakes in the first place. Moreover, negotiating without mistakes means that deal breakthroughs become routine. Remember that the basic reason for entering negotiations is to make a deal and to make it a good deal. This book is designed to enable you to negotiate without costly mistakes, to avoid dealbreakers, to make deal breakthroughs, and, thus, to make good deals.

CHAPTER 1

The One-Track Mind

Dangers of a Preset Mental Framework

> *Well begun is half done.*
>
> Aristotle

> *Chaos often breeds life,*
> *when order breeds habit.*
>
> Henry Brook Adams

A few years ago, I was one of several panel speakers at a large gathering. The speaker who preceded me began his presentation by asking the audience to refrain from questions or comments until he was finished. He then began reading his carefully typed speech, word for word. About halfway through the reading, a persistent member of the audience, who had been constantly waving his arm, was finally allowed to speak. Another member of the audience joined in, and a ten-minute free-for-all discussion ensued. When things finally quieted down, the interrupted speaker was unable to locate precisely where he had departed from his prepared text. His face reddened. He coughed nervously a couple of times, made a few off-the-cuff parting remarks, collected his papers, and sat down—totally defeated.

This frustrated speaker had evidently never learned the lesson of Napoleon, that is, the lesson of the military commander who was so brilliant before he met his Waterloo.

THE LESSON OF NAPOLEON

Napoleon once explained to a conquered opponent why he (the opponent) had been defeated:

> I will tell you the mistake you are always making.
> . . . You *draw up your plans the day before battle,*
> when you do not yet know your adversary's movements, or what positions you will have to occupy.[*]
> (Emphasis added.)

The lesson of Napoleon is *flexibility*. In order to succeed in any confrontation, you must be able to adapt to

---

[*]Emil Ludwig, *Napoleon* (New York: Garden City Publishing Co., 1926), 341.

changing conditions. This principle holds true in fighting a battle, in giving a speech, and in conducting negotiations.

Negotiation is a freewheeling activity in which anything can, and often does, happen. It is vital that you enter with a mind-set that will enable you to react instantly to the unexpected in such a way as to continuously move toward your negotiation objectives. You do that by placing yourself mentally in a position to determine quickly and to implement quickly the best means of persuasion for each specific negotiating situation that arises.

That is impossible when you are committed to a preestablished mental frame. If you are locked into a strategy beforehand, like the unfortunate panel speaker, you will be unable to adapt your approach when unanticipated obstacles emerge. Furthermore, a skilled opponent—like Napoleon and the mere mortals whom you might encounter across the negotiating table—will discover your rigidity and act immediately to take full advantage of your mental weakness and derail your one-track mind.

In fact, many negotiators make themselves vulnerable in just this way. They prepare, enter, and conduct negotiations with a preset mental frame that may include not only an established order for the issues to be discussed, but also an order for discussing the various relevant facets of each issue. They, thus, become a train running along one mental track, with no option for turning left or right to avoid the obstacles and pitfalls that are virtually certain to occur along the way during every negotiation of consequence.

RECOGNIZING AND EXPLOITING RIGIDITY

I was able to take advantage of this sort of one-track mind-set when negotiating a very substantial case involving numerous valuations of both raw and improved land, stock in both public and privately owned corporations, and legal interpretations of trusts and a will. It is human nature to attempt to arrange a collection of complicated issues like these into some orderly sequence during preparations and to try to enter and conduct negotiations in that preset order. I was, therefore, able to anticipate that my (two) opponents would be prone to just such an arrangement and to proceed accordingly.

After the usual opening pleasantries were exchanged, I immediately began probing for any evidence of a preset mental frame. The dialogue went something like this:

ILICH: Where do you want to start?

OPPONENTS: Let's start with all the real estate issues.

ILICH: You want to take the raw land first, then the improved property? (*I'm probing.*)

OPPONENTS: Yes. We'd definitely prefer that.

ILICH: Then where shall we go?

OPPONENTS: The corporations.

ILICH: Take the private ones first, then the public ones?

OPPONENTS: Public first. Private next. Then we can move on to the trust issues.

ILICH: And finish with the will question?

OPPONENTS: Uh huh.

Notice that my opponents had a very clear picture of the order they wanted to follow. Their use of the word *definitely* was a tipoff. Correcting me on the order of negotiating the value of the corporate stock issues was a further tipoff. Notice also how I used questions to draw out their mental frame. Questions are excellent tools for that purpose.

By extrapolating, I could, even at that very early juncture of the proceedings, assume that when we commenced negotiating each particular issue, my opponents would have preestablished an order of discussion. They would be likely, for instance, to have decided how and when they wanted to discuss all the facets concerning every one of the main issues. For example, on each issue involving valuing improved real estate, they would discuss (1) income and expense generated from the property, (2) physical condition of the property, (3) location of the property, (4) existing and future competition in the area of the property, and (5) taxes, in that same order.

As sound as my assumption about their mind-set might have been, however, I wanted a little more conclusive evidence before countering with my strategic response (remember Napoleon). One approach would have been to test immediately. Once my opponents announced they were ready to begin negotiating a particular issue, I could declare that a legitimate reason existed to start with another. But I decided to adopt that tactic *after* negotiations commenced because I wanted to be *certain* a preset mental frame existed and, furthermore, I wanted my opponents mental train to be a ways down the track and picking up steam before I derailed it.

When a person enters into a negotiation with a preset mental frame and is allowed to successfully commence and initially conduct the negotiation with that mental frame, a certain momentum is built up that makes it much more difficult for the person to get his or her mind back on track once it runs into a derailing obstacle. (Remember the speaker interrupted in the middle of his presentation.)

So it was with my two opponents. We quickly disposed of the first two issues involving the value of raw land. But just as we were about to begin negotiating the value of a third parcel of unimproved land, I suddenly announced that I preferred to jump to the valuation of the stock of one of the privately owned corporations because the land we had just valued was one of the assets of that corporation. My opponents objected. I tactfully persisted, pointing out that the issues were related and that it would be much easier to value the corporate stock now that we had arrived at a value of one of the assets of the corporation. My opponents exchanged nervous glances, then reluctantly agreed.

It was obvious from their behavior that they had locked in mentally to a preestablished negotiation sequence. Having imprisoned themselves, they effectively left the negotiations under my control. Continually throughout the proceedings, I was able to derail their strategy and keep them off balance and off schedule. Their resulting mental chaos allowed me to attain my negotiating objectives on virtually every material negotiable issue.

MORE WISDOM FROM NAPOLEON

Napoleon enlightened the same luckless adversary on the essence of successful military strategy:

> But for my part, I *never* issue orders *long in advance,* and am especially cautious over-night. At peep of day, I send out my scouts, survey the field for myself, and keep my troops in mass formation as long as I am still in doubt. . . . Then I hurl myself on the enemy, attacking him *wherever the ground makes attack most favorable.** (Emphasis added.)

---

*Emil Ludwig, *Napoleon* (New York: Garden City Publishing Co., 1926), 341.

Every negotiator should consider very carefully Napoleon's wise words when preparing for, entering into, and conducting any negotiation. Napoleon never preset his battle strategy. He simply prepared thoroughly for a battle he knew was coming and conceived his battle strategy *right on the spot after carefully determining what his opponent would do.* It was, therefore, virtually impossible for his opponent to determine with any degree of accuracy what moves Napoleon would make during the course of the battle. Napoleon, on the other hand, knew with a great degree of accuracy what his opponent's moves would be.

FLEXIBILITY ALSO MEANS BEING READY

Even the best laid plans often go astray. Many years ago in a busy, crowded, Chicago courtroom, I witnessed an illustration of that truism.

As scheduled, two lawyers began arguing a motion before the judge. The judge glanced at the case file before him, then glared menacingly at the two lawyers before shouting angrily: "You two back here again?! I thought I told you last time to settle this case!" He then stood up and flung the file across the courtroom over the heads of the other lawyers waiting their turn to argue motions. Papers flew all over the room, but the bulk of the file stayed intact, hitting the wall with a thud and falling heavily to the hard wooden floor. The judge, by now his face bright red with anger, pointed toward where the file had landed and bellowed: "Go back there and don't come back until you've reached a settlement." The stunned lawyers complied meekly.

The abused lawyers were set for battle in the formally structured arena of the courtroom. Probably the last thing on their minds was that they would be forced into negotiating a settlement. One wonders which of the lawyers was better able to adapt to the changed conditions—get his derailed train back on track—and succeed at the negotiations. Was either one of them flexible enough to be the "Napoleon" of this conflict?

The story of the irascible Chicago judge illustrates that not only is a preset mental frame a severe liability during negotiations, it is destructive for anyone whose business includes negotiating or, in other ways, resolving disputes. In an often turbulent, combative, and unsettled world, negotiation can be a highly volatile and completely unpredictable affair. Fortunately, the art of negotiation can be learned. The first step is acquiring the right mental attitude.

GETTING YOUR MIND RIGHT

Successful negotiation entails the ability to first determine through observation and analysis the best means of persuasion for any given negotiating situation and to then put that persuasive approach into practice at the appropriate time. In most negotiating situations, there are several options available, including perhaps the one preset in a negotiator's mind. There is, however, only one *best* option, which must be selected and applied even if it was not the one expected.

The only way to accomplish this task is to prepare for, enter into, and conduct the negotiation with complete mental freedom, permitting your mind the widest degree of flexibility.

Napoleon's approach to battle is precisely the right approach to any negotiation. Prepare for each negotiable issue thoroughly, know it backward and forward, and *be ready to discuss it backward, forward, or any other way*! Then you are not really concerned with the order in which the issues are to be discussed or, for that matter, the order of discussion of the various facets within each issue. Your mental frame is such that you can skip to any facet of the negotiation with ease. It's virtually impossible for your opponent to derail you.

RIGIDITY IS PREDICTABILITY

What better place to go for an example of inflexible mind-set (and how to exploit it) than to the military. General George C. Marshall is remembered for the Marshall Plan to rebuild Europe after the Second World War. The plan, which bares his name, was instituted while Marshall was Secretary of State under President Harry Truman. He demonstrated the perceptions of a great negotiator, however, when he was a young lieutenant serving in the Philippines. Marshall's company was due for an inspection, and he bet a fellow lieutenant that he could name in advance three trivial faults the inspecting officer would find and three grave errors in tactics Marshall would commit that the inspector would fail to note.

Marshall predicted that the inspector would find that one soldier needed a shave, another had unbuttoned buttons on his blouse, and a third was without his bayonet. Marshall further predicted that the inspecting officer would fail to notice that Marshall marched his men in a column of four toward the enemy instead of dispersing them, sent a corporal at the head of a squad toward the enemy without instructions, and attacked up the face of a hill instead of through a nearby wooded area that would have provided his men with cover. Marshall was correct on all six predictions.

He had learned that the rigid mind-set of the inspector always focused on certain small areas, to such a degree that all else was practically invisible. This perceptive insight permitted Marshall to get away with major errors by offering the inspector what he was predisposed to see. It's possible that Marshall could have frustrated the inspecting officer and earned a perfect score by eliminating those expected minor errors. But it is just as likely that a thwarted inspector would have had to find *something* and so would have picked up some other irregularity. The point is that by knowing the rigid mind-set of his "adversary," Marshall was in control of the situation and had the flexibility to accomplish his goals.

TAKING ADVANTAGE OF RIGIDITY

On occasion, despite your best efforts, you will be unable to shake opponents out of their preset mental frames. It's almost as if they say to themselves: "We are going to follow the agenda we've mentally prepared no matter what!" Don't despair. They are still very vulnerable, because, as with the young George Marshall's inspector, a serious drawback of a preset mental frame is the danger of becoming predictable.

Let's return to the case of the two overly structured negotiators who had preplanned our entire negotiation schedule. Suppose my opponents had refused to jump the tracks and had not agreed, at my urging, to deviate from their preset schedule and take up the issue of the value of the corporate stock after negotiating the value of the first two raw parcels of land. If other attempts at disrupting their flow had also failed, I would have had to alter my negotiating strategy to one of predicting my opponents moves.

Because they were locked into a preset mental frame, they would have been very predictable indeed. Their arguments, their positions, their persuasive techniques, all would likely adhere to a recognizable pattern. Because I would have been able to anticipate every aspect of their performance, I would have been able to direct, counter, and manipulate to achieve my negotiation objectives. In short, like General Marshall, I would have been in control—and without my opponents realizing I was in control.

To sum up, when confronted with negotiating opponents who are afflicted with mental rigidity, make their condition terminal. You can take control of the negotiations by either disrupting their preset framework or by anticipating their every move. Your flexibility in response to their rigidity means you are in charge. Either approach is better than slavishly following your opponents' schedule, thus negotiating on their terms, or stubbornly locking horns, thus running the risk of preventing any meaningful progress. Flexibility defeats rigidity.

FINAL ADVICE

Although flexibility in negotiation is essential, getting ready to negotiate requires paying attention to a few fundamental rules. Any negotiation—large or small, simple or complex—should be approached in the following manner:

1. Prepare well. Know intimately both your side and your opponent's side. Napoleon knew all the details relevant to his military campaigns, including when every horse in a cavalry squadron would have to be re-shod and how many loaves of bread a field bakery could turn out in a day.

2. Have a good, basic, but general plan of strategies and techniques you anticipate using—but avoid any preset, specific format as to when and how you will use them. Make those decisions as the negotiation develops, right on the spot, as you deem the situations dictate. You will be applying the lesson of Napoleon.

3. Always be cognizant that anything can and does happen in negotiation. Condition yourself to that attitude so that when unexpected and unanticipated events occur, you will be able to adjust easily and effectively. Change is the only constant when mind is pitted against mind.

By adhering to these principles, you will put yourself in a strong negotiating position. You will be able to accurately assess the negotiating situation, select the best means of persuasion, and implement your choice effectively. Your flexibility will protect you from becoming predictable and, thus, compromising your negotiating position.

CHAPTER 2

Who Can Say "Yes"?

Knowing Who Has Final Negotiating Authority

Assumption is the mother of screw up.

Angelo Donghia

What we've got here is a failure to communicate.

Donn Pearce
Cool Hand Luke
(screenplay)

Failure to hit the bull's-eye is never the fault of the target.

Gilbert Arland

In virtually every negotiation, one individual possesses the responsibility and authority to make all final decisions relative to the negotiation. That person might not be present for some or any of the negotiating sessions. You must reach that person to attain the quickest and most effective results. Failure to do so can lead to harsh and devastating consequences. President Jimmy Carter learned this truth to his and the nation's sorrow in 1980.

THE LESSON OF THE IRANIAN HOSTAGES

You will remember that 54 Americans were held hostage in Iran for 14 months during the Carter administration. The entire nation was preoccupied with their fate. During the first ten months of the hostages' captivity, however, the United States was negotiating for their release with the wrong people, that is the secular, titular leaders of Iran rather than the religious figures, who held the real power. As a result, no meaningful progress in negotiations occurred. Nearly a year of valuable time had been wasted by not dealing with the people who could say "yes" to the negotiating goal of getting the hostages home. This failure not only prolonged the suffering of the hostages and their families, it depressed the American public and severely damaged (perhaps fatally) the Carter administration.

The initial mistake in the Iranian hostage crisis is in a way understandable: U. S. leaders are used to dealing with governments, not religious figures. Nonetheless, the experience illustrates the danger of *assuming* you know who is really in charge on the other side. While your negotiations are unlikely to carry the global impact of releasing hostages from foreign nationals, they are still vital to your interests. Therefore, you must avoid the all-to-common mistake of negotiating with whoever happens to show up to represent the opposition at the negotiation sessions.

Always ask yourself these crucial questions:

1. Do any of the persons with whom I am negotiating possess final authority to bind the agreement?
2. If not, who does?

AN EXAMPLE CLOSER TO HOME

Getting to the person who can say "yes" was critical to success when Pennzoil was negotiating a merger with Getty Oil a few years ago. It was proposed to Hugh Liedtke, chairman of Pennzoil and a very experienced, shrewd negotiator, that a series of "structured meetings" be held first.

> "What on earth is that?" Liedtke demanded. "Well, they (lawyers and investment bankers) want to present to you an outline of what to talk to Mr. Getty (Gordon Getty, son of the legendary J. Paul Getty) about, and then they'll go up and review it with Mr. Getty." *"Like hell they will!"* Liedtke bellowed. "I'm going to deal directly with Mr. Getty and I'm not going to deal with third parties. I don't want them telling Mr. Getty what *I* think of what *I'm* offering. I want to sit right across the table from him and tell him myself so there won't be any questions about who said what."*

THE HAZARDS OF DEALING WITH THE WRONG PEOPLE

The cases just cited illustrate the major hazards of not negotiating directly with the individual who has final

---

*Thomas Petzinger, Jr., *Oil and Honor* (New York: G. P. Putnam's Sons, 1987), 152–53.

authority to make the deal. You may encounter the following situations:

1. Not dealing with the person who can say "yes" means the negotiations may not progress (the lesson of the Iranian hostages).

2. The people you're dealing with may not *accurately* pass on what you are proposing to the person who does have final negotiating authority. (Liedtke alluded to this danger when he declared that he didn't want there to "be any questions about who said what.")

3. You will not be able to use your negotiating skills directly where they can do the most good—on the person who can say "yes."

4. You will not be able to observe and "read" the person who can say "yes," which will obviously inhibit your negotiating effectiveness.

5. The person who can say "yes" will be insulated from the heat of negotiations, thus permitting your principal opponent to make decisions with little or no mental pressure.

Of course, knowing what the hazards are is one thing; avoiding them is another—first you have to find out who is in charge before you can insist on dealing with the right person. Hugh Liedtke knew from the start and was able to get to the man on top right away; the U.S. State Department, for all its experience and expertise, took ten months.

LOOKING FOR THE "YES" PERSON

Over the years, I've found different approaches that work in different situations. One of the most unusual approaches turned up in a very common setting.

Don't Let Them Double Team You

Early in my career, I was negotiating with two lawyers, both in their sixties and both very experienced. The negotiation was complicated with a number of issues, and numerous sessions were held. Each session would be handled entirely by one lawyer, with the other remaining silent and impassive as a sphinx guarding a pharaoh's tomb. Decisions were made solely by the lawyer actively conducting the negotiation. But at each subsequent session, the two would reverse roles—the silent lawyer became the negotiator; his partner became the sphinx.

The difficulty with this arrangement was that frequently matters decided by one lawyer were reopened by the other at the next meeting. Even at this early stage in my career, I realized that by taking two steps forward at one session and two steps back at the next, I would not get very far. More frustrating was my inability to determine conclusively, although I had my suspicions, which of the two lawyers was really calling the shots.

The solution was to convince the partners that they both had to be involved in each session. I reasoned that if I saw them both in action, side-by-side, I would be better able to determine who actually had final negotiating authority. Faced with my insistence that the current arrangement would produce only stalemate and unwanted litigation, my opponents reluctantly agreed. After several sessions, it became clear which lawyer was in charge: he began talking more than his partner and even correcting him. With the identity of the "yes" man established, the negotiations progressed smoothly.

Negotiating with more than one person is common. The problem of determining who has the ultimate authority to make decisions is complicated, however, when a variation on this situation occurs, namely, when you are negotiating with a person or persons representing a principal who is not present. A lawyer representing a client would be a typical example. In many of these cases, it is not possible to negotiate directly with the client (as Hugh Liedtke was able to do with Gordon Getty). This is especially true when the negotiation concerns settlement of litigation where an attorney would not care to expose a client to the attorney for the other side. In this situation, you will be forced to proceed through the attorney to get to the "yes" person.

Just Ask

The simplest and surest way to determine who possesses the final negotiating authority is to ask. Often your opponents will forthrightly identify the person who has the authority to make binding decisions. On occasion, however, they may mislead you deliberately, perhaps from a human reluctance to admit a lack of importance. Your opponent's deception might also be a strategic ploy to induce you to disclose your negotiating position to the "wrong" person, allowing the individual empowered to say "yes" the luxury of unpressured assessment and response. Thus, be sure to ask who is in charge, but be sure to verify the answer you receive with your own observations.

Titles Can Be Tricky

The person with the highest title may not be the one with the final say in the negotiations. I once negotiated a contract directly with a corporate president, a person one would ordinarily assume would have the authority to make binding agreements. But this executive was tentative, always suggesting when it came time to make a decision that he preferred to think the matter over. At each subsequent session, he would propose a modification of our tentative agreement. As the negotiation continued, a company vice president sometimes attended but participated in the discussions only on a limited basis. It became readily apparent, however, from the president's frequent glances at the vice president that the subordinate was calling the shots. As it turned out, the president was deferring to the vice president's superior technical knowledge in that aspect of the negotiation. Once I understood the situation, I directed my strategy toward favorably influencing the vice president.

Another reason why titles can be misleading is that in many large institutions titles have become almost meaningless. Banks, for example, have multiple vice presidents and even executive vice presidents, who may have no significant authority. I, therefore, usually ask, at the initial "get acquainted" period that proceeds most negotiations, what the duties/responsibilities of the titled persons are. Although some people will exaggerate their importance, the answers I get to that simple question—when combined with other relevant information and filtered by my experience—often help determine the true extent of each individual's authority.

Age Doesn't Matter

Never be misled by age. Seniority no longer denotes authority. You cannot allow yourself to equate gray hair with power; the younger member on your opponent's team might have the final say in the negotiations. In fact, many young business and professional people are the negotiators in charge today, when they have proven they get results.

Be aware, as well, that the younger opponent might be in authority even if the older member of the team appears to be. Often age receives its deference merely out of politeness. This may especially be true when the individuals are related. The son or daughter might run the family business built up by the parent and seek parental approval of decisions reached during negotiation out of respect, although no such approval is actually needed.

The difficulty of knowing who has the final say in a family business is illustrated in the story of financial titan J. P. Morgan and the Rockefellers. Morgan controlled the production and manufacture of steel after buying out Andrew Carnegie but was still in great need of iron ore. Unfortunately for Morgan, American ore fields were controlled by John D. Rockefeller. The men detested each other. But Morgan, desperate for the iron ore, arranged a meeting with Rockefeller, at which time Morgan was informed that John D. was retired from business and that his son, John Jr., then 27, would handle the negotiations. As it turned out, the old man was still very much in control and using his son as a front man to feel out Morgan and gain an advantage in the transactions. In this case, parental approval was definitely required.

Appearances Can Be Deceiving

Just as the oldest member of the negotiating team might not be the one with the greatest authority, the individual with the most expensive suit, fashionable accoutrements, stylish haircut, ostentatious jewelry, or commanding presence may not be the dominant member of the group. That seems obvious, but certain physical signs have come to be associated with power, and those perceptual habits can be hard to break. I was fortunate to receive a valuable lesson in the deception of appearances early in my career.

When I was a young attorney, I was asked to accompany one of the firm's partners on a trip to have some contracts signed by a client. We traveled to a farm near our home base in Chicago. As we approached the old, wooden-frame farm house, a man slowly came to meet us from an old barn, wiping grease from his hands as he drew near. He was unshaven and wore dirty overalls and a dirty, grease-smeared baseball hat. I took him for a hired hand. Of course, he was the man we had come to see. We exchanged a few pleasantries, he signed the documents we had brought, and then he returned to the barn to, he said, finish tinkering with an old tractor. The "hired hand," I learned, was the owner of a very substantial company and worth many, many millions of dollars.

Take It All In

The most reliable and, thus, the wisest way to determine who possesses final negotiating authority is to consider a combination of all the relevant factors I have just discussed and include in that mix, most importantly, your experience with people. Factor in, as well, your prenegotiation research and investigation of your opponents. In most instances, you will be able to conclude correctly the true extent of your opponent's authority, perhaps before the negotiation commences.

Very helpful, too, is a keen sense of observation. Frederick Foerster wrote: "If you don't use your eyes for seeing, you will need them for weeping." Watch your opponents; see how they conduct themselves. Are they hesitant, uncertain, tentative? That may mean they lack the authority to make the decisions necessary to bind the negotiation. Are they bold, decisive, confident? Those who possess authority usually are. Your opponents' attitudes will give them away. Observe them carefully.

I was once negotiating several contracts with a pair of attorneys. One attorney conducted the negotiations while the other remained silent. When it came to decision-making time, the passive partner flashed hand signals to the active partner on whether to agree or disagree on each particular point. Fortunately, the signaling attorney was just within my peripheral vision, and I was able to observe their technique. The silent partner was the one with the real power. He had neatly removed himself from the heat of discussions, providing himself with the luxury—until I caught him—of making decisions on the issues in a calmer, more deliberative mental state. Obviously, I would have done a lot of "weeping" had I not been able to detect this arrangement very early in the negotiations.

In another case, I had to determine which of three people had the authority to say "yes." One clue was the location of the sessions; often these are held in the office of the one who holds the power, since "subordinates" would usually go to that office for meetings of importance. I knew from experience, however, that this clue could be misleading because negotiations are frequently held in the office of the person doing the bulk of the work, although that individual might not be the one who could make the deal.

I, therefore, decided to observe carefully my three opponents in action before drawing any conclusions as to who was in charge. I was looking for the five telltale signs of dominance:

1. Who spoke or acted with authority?
2. Did one interrupt the others?
3. Did one overrule the others?
4. Who asked the bulk of the questions?
5. Who openly contested any of my assertions?

Initially, none of the three men seemed to be dominant. But then they gave it away. I noticed that the man sitting at the desk (it was his office) and the colleague on his left would each sneak a glance at the man on his right when advocating a strong position. And the man on the left would nod ever so slightly. That was the tipoff that he had the power to say "yes."

Control Your Use of Pen and Paper

Two of your greatest negotiating assets are your eyes. Don't waste them on your own notes; don't become a slave to pen and paper. Lawyers are particularly prone to whipping out a legal pad and writing down virtually everything said during the negotiation—and missing much vital information in the process. It is better to pay attention to your opponents' body language (and to be aware of your own). The way a person moves, sits, smiles, frowns, holds his or her hands, and even coughs tells a lot. For instance, does your nervous cough indicate a lack of confidence in yourself or your negotiating position? Are your opponent's arms folded across his or her chest? That may signal a defensive mental frame. Are you sitting with your hands out in front, the tips of your fingers touching so as to form a steeple? Steepling connotes a confident mental state. An observant negotiator concentrating on these and many other body signs, rather than on making notes, can pick up a great deal of valuable information.

Consequently, if you write anything at all during the course of the negotiation, note only the agreements reached and any data and materials promised to the other negotiating party. Other than that, forget the pen and paper. Concentrate fully on your opponent and the subject matter at hand. I often walk away from even a complicated negotiating session with out having written a single word. I usually jot down any notes *immediately after* the session; only then do I shift my focus from my opponent and the negotiation itself.

Thwart Your Opponent's Observations

When I leave a session, I am particularly careful to avoid doing anything that would risk upsetting agreements reached during negotiations. And that includes controlling my face. An associate and I once conducted a negotiation in an office that was right next to the exit to the street. As we were leaving the building, I warned my partner not to show the delight we were feeling after the hours of hard work in the just-completed session. I knew our opponents would be watching us carefully as we walked past their office window, and I didn't want the broad smiles we were holding inside to break out and give them second thoughts about the agreements we had made but that had not yet been put in writing. Backing away from oral agreements is, unfortunately, a common occurrence in negotiation, especially if one party, already crammed with self-doubt, has his or her suspicions raised by the other party's premature celebrations. So enjoy your victories in private.

Watch for the Reluctant Authority

It is not uncommon to encounter a negotiator who has final authority but, for one reason or another, refuses to exercise it. This situation is not only frustrating but potentially hazardous to your objectives because you may have been focusing your attention on the wrong individual.

On one occasion, I was representing the executors of a large estate in a negotiation with the Internal Revenue Service. The IRS agent in charge of the case was accompanied by his supervisor. Supervisors routinely sit in during negotiations, but principally to audit their agents' effectiveness, not to participate in the negotiation. The agent, therefore, has the authority to make all the decisions. Early in this particular negotiation, however, I sensed that the supervisor was really the one in charge, even though he was not contributing to the discussions. Little things tipped me off, like the agent's nervous glance at the supervisor when decision time arrived. Although he had formal authority, the agent was too weak an individual to take responsibility in a case involving many millions of dollars. I was forced to redirect my presentation to the supervisor; he was the one who, by default, could say "yes."

NEGOTIATION STRATEGIES

In the Iranian hostage crisis, a careful and skillful probe by the Carter administration during the early stages of the negotiations would have revealed that the Iranian religious leaders, principally the Ayatollah Khomeini, had the real decision-making authority. Armed with this intelligence, the U.S. negotiators would have had several viable options. The best would have been to deal directly with Khomeini.

Dealing directly with the person who has the final say is always the most desirable approach. However, one cannot always follow a straight path to the target. If that is the case, then the negotiator must select another mode of attack.

Using Conduits

Obviously, it would have been impossible for the State Department to deal directly with Khomeini. They might, however, have been able to do the next best thing, namely, persuade one or more of the other religious leaders— preferably a person or persons very close to the Ayatollah and with some influence over him—to participate in the negotiations. They would have been direct conduits to the man in charge and so offer a better hope for success.

Using others to reach the person with final negotiating authority is not without its drawbacks and, therefore, is recommended only when it is impossible to negotiate directly with the one who can say "yes." There is no assurance, for example, that those acting as conduits will be able to convey your thoughts as accurately, forcefully, and skillfully as you did during the negotiating session. In addition, your conduits might deliberately dilute or color your message for purposes of their own.

Nevertheless, negotiating with conduits is less risky than dealing with people who have virtually no decision-making authority. Recall that the Carter administration wasted ten months talking to secular, titular leaders in Iran. Not only were these people unlikely to convey the U.S. message accurately because of their philosophical differences with Khomeini, they would be competing with him and his followers for power in Iran. This rivalry would substantially, and perhaps irrevocably, make it virtually impossible to attain any meaningful progress in negotiations.

Applying an Oblique Approach

Essentially, you will face one of three possible negotiating situations. The person who can say "yes" will be (1) present at the negotiation and participating, (2) present but not participating, or (3) not present (as in the Iranian hostage crisis). Consider again a case I cited earlier in which I identified the man in charge as the silent one who nodded "ever so slightly" as his two colleagues negotiated aggressively and glanced cautiously (and surreptitiously) at him for confirmation of their positions. He was the object of my attention, even as I continued to deal with his more vocal subordinates.

During a substantial portion of the negotiation, I articulated my thoughts to influence *him* while I was actually looking at and speaking to the other two. The documents I submitted to his colleagues in support of my positions were designed to convince him, not them. As the negotiation progressed, he began displaying a lack of interest in many of the matters raised by the junior members of his team. He even reprimanded one of them for being too "technical" when that unfortunate man contested a point I was making about a court case. I knew then that not only had I accurately pegged the "yes" man, but my oblique attack strategy was correct.

Gauging the Attorney's Influence

Many times you will find yourself negotiating with a lawyer who is representing a client. In most of these situations, it is not possible to deal directly with the client. Accordingly, I have discovered that the most productive approach is to gauge the strength of the attorney in relation to the strength of the client. If, for example, the attorney is dominant, the client is more likely to go along with the attorney's recommendations. If, on the other hand, the client is dominant, then the client will make all the relevant decisions. Determining who is in charge entails some investigation, of course, but should not be too difficult. First determine the background of the client.

Most people who hire attorneys to handle their negotiations are themselves unschooled in the technicalities and complexities of the law. Hence, if the client in question is not a lawyer, that client will be dependent upon the advice of the representing attorney in the negotiations. Although technically the client has the final decision-making authority, the lawyer is the one who has the power to say "yes."

A client may have the training, experience, or strength

of personality to make all final decisions relative to the negotiations, including those that overrule the attorney. Try to determine whether the client behind the negotiation is a lawyer, a high executive in a corporation (chairman, president, executive vice president), or a business owner (especially of a large firm requiring strong management). Chances are that such a person, not the attorney, will be calling the shots. In that case, you must direct the substance of your message to the client, even though he or she is not actually present at the negotiations. The information you present at the negotiation, especially any written data, should be tailored not for the attorney with whom you are negotiating, but for the dominant client. For instance, if you are negotiating the sale of a business with excellent annual net profits, it would be wise to prepare an annual history of net profits and request that the document be forwarded to the client for personal review. The negotiating attorney becomes a conduit who can relay your positions to the person (the client) who has the authority to say "yes."

Beating the Double Team

On occasion, you will encounter a situation where final negotiating authority is held by more than one person. Members of corporate committees, for example, may possess joint decision-making authority. You will find that the same can be true in negotiations with certain government agencies, family businesses, partnerships, and joint ventures. However, in virtually every one of these situations, a dominant personality will emerge. Your task is to identify the strongest, most forceful individual, the one who is apt to exercise the greatest influence over the others on the negotiating team when it comes to decision time. You should direct the substance of your thoughts toward that dominant person, even though you may be looking at and talking to the others in the party. Your strategic goal here is to forcefully and accurately impress your positions on the dominant person's mind. You, thus, will have acquired a strong ally who will help you persuade the remaining holders of decision-making authority as to the merits of your arguments. In that way, you will be able to reach (and convince) *all* the people who can say "yes."

REACHING THE "YES" PERSON

To recap, your principal goal in negotiation must be to establish a direct line of communication with the individual who can give you what you want. A substantial amount of valuable time, energy, and money can be wasted by negotiating with people who do not have the authority to make binding decisions, as was shown in the Iranian hostage situation.

An open mind and a keen, observant eye can rather quickly determine who has decision-making authority. You can then select the proper strategic approach to reach and persuade the one with authority to say "yes" to decisions favorable to your negotiation objectives. Indeed, had the Carter administration been talking to the religious leaders at or near the onset of the crisis, the hostages very well could have been released much sooner and President Carter's chances of winning re-election substantially improved.

Talking to the "wrong" opponents is always a fatal flaw!

CHAPTER 3

Machiavelli Revisited

Using Negotiating Power at the Right Time

The meek shall inherit the earth, but the strong shall retain the mineral rights.

Anonymous

The saying that knowledge is power is not quite true. Used knowledge is power.

Dr. Edward E. Free

Immense power is acquired by assuring yourself in your secret reveries that you were born to control affairs.

Andrew Carnegie

Andrew Carnegie was one of the cruelest taskmasters American industry has ever known. He was also one of the shrewdest negotiators of his time because he possessed an unerring knowledge of human nature. Carnegie had a reputation in the business community for ferocity, which he earned through his jungle methods of trampling out competition. The time came, however, when the tiger wanted to retire—but at his own price. He knew the only person who could put together a deal to pay his price was J. Pierpont Morgan, the great banker and financial genius. Morgan hated Carnegie's mode of doing business, but Carnegie saw that as an asset rather than a liability.

Carnegie realized that his ruthless business reputation gave him substantial negotiating power if wisely used in a timely way. So he boldly set out on a campaign to literally *force* Morgan to buy him out. He publicly announced a series of daring new business ventures— that he intended to build a gigantic rod mill in Pittsburgh, bringing in raw materials from the Great Lakes on his own ships and his own railroad. Carnegie even let contracts for a $12-million tube plant on Lake Erie.

As he anticipated, his expansion plans threw the steel and iron industry into a turmoil. His panicked competitors rushed to Morgan and begged him to organize the industry into one company. They wanted Morgan to buy out Carnegie before Carnegie ruined them all. Morgan reluctantly agreed. He, too, had steel, iron, and railroad interests that needed to be protected. He organized the first billion-dollar corporation, U. S. Steel, and bought out Carnegie for the tiger's price of over $217 million. Carnegie's success was a classic case of the effective use of power in negotiations.

POWER IS IN THE MIND OF THE BEHOLDER

A person with a loaded gun and the will to shoot is an elemental (and all too familiar) example of power: the person with the gun compels others to do what he or she wants. Fortunately, negotiators normally don't carry tangible power-representing devices, like guns, to win their way. They have to prevail by essentially the written and spoken word, by use of tactics and strategies that will persuade the other party.

Anything or everything that will motivate the opponent favorably toward the negotiator's objectives constitutes negotiating power. In the Carnegie-Morgan case, the industrialist's tigerlike business reputation was his power. Competitors feared him. In a sense, Carnegie's financial strength and his record of using it to crush the competition was the loaded gun, held by a man with the will to shoot it, pointed at the head of Morgan and his group. But negotiating power is not always so stark or brutal.

Consider the case of an antique-car owner approached by a prospective buyer. The owner gains the impression from the buyer's tone and attitude that the buyer is very interested in acquiring the car. The buyer's strong desire is the loaded gun. It can be translated into negotiating power by the owner because that desire motivates the buyer favorably toward what the owner wants: a good price for the car. The owner can employ tactics to use that power. He might, for instance, spend a substantial amount of time showing off the car to the buyer, conducting sales negotiations while standing next to the car or even while sitting in the car, thus keeping the car in the forefront of the buyer's mind and feeding his desire. Used in this manner, as a tangible prop to promote and facilitate sales, the car becomes what is known as a "demonstrative exhibit."

In addition, the car owner is effectively employing the highly productive technique of *repetition* (which I will discuss in more detail later in this chapter). As the buyer sits in the car, looking around, feeling the upholstery, and listening to the owner talk, his senses of sight, touch, and hearing are being assaulted; his already-strong

desire is being stimulated. Negotiating in this atmo-
sphere, the owner can use his power on the mind of the
prospective buyer and motivate him to pay the owner's
price. Never lose sight of the fact that negotiation is
mind versus mind, and it is your opponent's mind you
must reach to accomplish your negotiating objectives.

Carnegie translated his tough business reputation
into tremendous negotiating power. The seller did the
same with the buyer's desire to own the antique car.
Reputation. Desire. Both completely intangible, wholly
within the human mind. It is because qualities such as
these are not visible as "loaded guns" that so many
negotiators fail to understand fully what constitutes
negotiating power. That failure, of course, often leads to
devastating results in negotiations.

Notice that both Carnegie and the antique-car seller
operated to heighten an emotional state of mind in their
opponents. Carnegie's public pronouncements of bold,
new business ventures played on the fear of his competitors and Morgan that he would ruin them. The car seller
elevated the buyer's desire by assaulting his senses.
Emotion is a mental response that in itself tends to
stimulate activity. Hence, when you tap into the emotions of your opponent, you may expect a definite and
most often positive reaction.

FEAR IS POWER

Of all the emotions, fear is the greatest motivator. People
fear many, many things. They fear financial loss, they
fear being embarrassed, they fear for their safety, for
their family's safety. The list is endless, but the response
is virtually always the same: alleviate the feeling. The
motivation of your opponent to remove the fear is what
you must translate into negotiating power.

I was at one time in charge of negotiating the sale of

a prime site for a branch bank. Approaching a bank with the site details and working to convince management to pay a top price would certainly be one way of tackling the matter and would be part of the normal negotiating process. But that method had only limited power. To substantially increase my power, I approached several banks with the site details and made certain that each bank knew a competitor might acquire the site. Power is useless unless its true extent is known. By making all the parties aware of the potential loss of the site to another, I enlisted fear as a major ally in my quest to obtain a top price.

The antique-car owner could have easily taken a similar approach and created great fear of loss in the prospective buyer. He might have tactfully let it slip (assuming it was true) that another prospective purchaser was very interested in the car. Moreover, it definitely would have been to the car owner's advantage to actively seek other potential buyers, once the first buyer had made contact, in order to enhance that fear. In this way, the owner would have exploited more fully his negotiating power.

KNOWING YOU HAVE POWER IS POWER

Consider how costly it would have been for Carnegie had he failed to realize that his tigerlike business reputation afforded him tremendous negotiating power. Indeed, he would have found it virtually impossible to motivate Morgan, a man who detested him, to make a deal at all, let alone on favorable terms. Moreover, failing to understand the *extent* of his power might have doomed the great industrialist to failure. Indeed, since what constitutes negotiating power is most often intangible and wholly within the mind, people frequently find it quite difficult to assess accurately the true nature and extent of their power. This problem especially plagues those inexperienced in the art of negotiation.

The "Power Think Time" Technique

The "power think time" technique is a device you can use to assess accurately the true extent of your negotiating power. Before the negotiations begin, simply isolate yourself from all distractions and concentrate on answering one question: *What do I possess or what can I do to motivate my opponent favorably towards my negotiating objectives?* Jot your conclusions down on paper so that you can later evaluate their validity. As the negotiations progress, remain alert to sources of power that you may have overlooked in the initial examination and to new sources that may emerge during the discussions.

I acquired an unexpected source of power late in the afternoon of one session after I had met with a corporate executive most of the morning and early afternoon. About 3 o'clock, he became noticeably very nervous, speaking more quickly and frequently glancing at his watch. Finally, he advised me that he had to catch a flight at 5 o'clock in order to make an important meeting. His tight schedule empowered me. Deadlines, even self-imposed deadlines, provide an important source of negotiating power (as I shall discuss later in this book). In this case, the closer we got to 5 o'clock, the more anxious my opponent became and the more inclined to make concessions favorable to my purposes.

Although you should always be alert to power opportunities, it is useful to schedule "power think time" periods. I have found it very beneficial to spend some "power think time" as soon as practical after each negotiating session. It is best not to wait too long because the mind has a tendency to quickly forget, especially the tiny clues that can add up to important power gains. Ten to fifteen minutes of uninterrupted thought concerning what just transpired during the session is often very valuable. Not infrequently, I discover possible sources of power that I had not detected during the heat of the discussions when I had to concentrate fully on the matters at hand. As I gained experience as a negotiator, incidentally, my "power think time" became more productive. It is an excellent negotiation tool.

The following illustrates the benefits of "power think time." I was negotiating with two agents of the Internal Revenue Service on behalf of a beleaguered taxpayer. The IRS negotiators were reluctant to make a final commitment on one of the major issues. Their hesitation appeared deliberate, not due to indecision, and was thus quite puzzling. I immediately asked myself one of the key questions in negotiation: What is their motive? Any meaningful progress depended on my finding an answer. As I thought about the matter, I came to the inescapable conclusion that the IRS had decided to make a "test case" on this issue; that is, they wanted a case they could successfully litigate to get a court decision that could be used as a favorable precedent when a similar issue arose with other taxpayers.

In order to motivate the IRS towards my client's position, I had to focus *not* on the merits of the issue, but on the worthiness of this particular taxpayer's situation as a test case. I had to convince my opponents that the IRS would *lose* in court and, therefore, get an unfavorable ruling that would be used by taxpayers in future cases against the government. The IRS's fear of losing the test case thus became my source of negotiating power. Properly directed, I was able to establish why my client's position was factually and legally correct, thereby undermining the government's confidence in their prospective test case and settling the issue to our satisfaction.

Note that fear, again, was the emotional trigger that motivated an opponent to move toward what was for me a favorable outcome. Fear is just a feeling, a state of mind, but it is also a very powerful force that can and should be translated into tremendous negotiating power.

USING THE POWER OF FEAR

Goldwyn's Clever Power Play

A somewhat novel use of fear in negotiation was employed by the late movie mogul Samuel Goldwyn. He wanted to replace the contract of popular actor David Niven with a new, more lucrative seven-year agreement, offering as incentive the lead in a film called *Raffles*. Niven refused to sign, hoping for an even better deal. During costume tests for another movie at Goldwyn's studio, Niven noticed a man hovering nearby, dressed like the lead character in *Raffles*, posing for still photographs. Niven approached the man and inquired what he was doing. The man, a young actor named Dana Andrews, told Niven he had just been signed by Goldwyn and instructed to report to the studio and pose for pictures in costume. Niven got the message. Fearing he would lose the part of Raffles, Niven quickly signed the new contract with Goldwyn.

The Duke-Reynolds Confrontation

The tobacco industry provides another illustration of the power of fear. James B. Duke was building his American Tobacco trust and was not too gentle on the competition, which included R. J. Reynolds. Duke summoned Reynolds to his hotel room to lay down the law. "I'll give you one million for two-thirds of your company," Duke told Reynolds, "or I'll break you. Take your choice."

Duke's heavy ultimatum was designed, of course, to force his adversary to capitulate or at least to negotiate out of fear. But Reynolds was one of those chosen few, made out of sterner stuff, who could stand up to Duke. Remaining unrattled, he replied: "My price is three million. Otherwise, for every dollar you cost me, I'm going to cost American Tobacco a hundred."

Both sides were now trying to use fear as a weapon to prevail over the other. Who would blink first? Well, Reynolds got his three million. Duke realized that Reynolds could and would make good on his threat. Fear of that concrete probability forced Duke to accede to Reynolds's demands.

TIMING IS EVERYTHING

The Bible teaches that there is a "time for every purpose."* In the contemporary world of negotiations, that includes a time to use power. Once you have determined *what* your negotiating power is, deciding *when* to apply it is the next step.

I once had a client who was seeking to rezone a large tract of land in order to develop a single-family residential complex. As it happened, one particular zoning official, through the force of his personality, clearly dominated the zoning board. His support was, therefore, essential. (Recall the lesson of Chapter 2: get to the person who can say "yes.") Unfortunately, the official was firmly opposed to the rezoning. His basic objection was not single-family use of the property, it was density. He preferred one home per acre; my client wanted two homes per acre. In this case, compromise was not possible, but there was always fear.

---

*Ecclesiastes 3:1.

I knew that the key official was very fearful of multifamily unit (apartment) development in the area. I also knew that my client had received offers from a developer to buy the land for multifamily units—and the developer was fully prepared to go to court if he were denied that use of the property. I intended to convey that information to the key official because it obviously constituted negotiating power. In reserve, I had the likelihood that my client could win a court challenge to an unfavorable zoning decision because his request was within the zoning ordinances of the community and because it could be established that the key official's opposition was based upon his personal beliefs and not on other development in the locale in question. In fact, property in the immediate area of my client's property had a density greater than one home per acre.

The question was one of timing. I could present *directly* to the zoning official *during* negotiations the information that litigation to obtain multifamily approval was in the offing. But he might become angry (as people frequently do when confronted with disturbing news), lash out at my client, and entrench himself firmly against the zoning request. Anger fosters confidence, even if short lived. You'll never see an angry person cowering, huddled up, shrinking, or trembling. Angry people react strongly, and I didn't want to run that risk with our targeted official. I, therefore, decided on the *indirect* approach. I leaked the information that a developer was interested in the property for multifamily unit (apartment) development should single-family zoning not be granted, and I did so in a way that was certain to get to the key official *before* we actually met. I anticipated that our man would still experience the fear, without attributing his feelings to me or my client, and, therefore, would spare us having to circumvent his anger.

My indirect approach was, of course, very similar to Carnegie's tactic of announcing his major new business ventures, because, in both cases, the "bad news" that instilled fear was conveyed prior to the actual negotiation. When I met with the zoning official, he immediately asked about the "rumors" of a multifamily unit developer's interest in the property. I confirmed the rumors, but told him that selling the land to the developer was the last thing my client desired. I further told him that if my client's zoning request was denied, he would have no other options. The reluctant official got the point, and our zoning request was approved.

In war, most battles are won by an indirect assault on the enemy's weakest points, not by a direct attack on the strongest defenses. This strategy forces the enemy to draw troops from its strongest points to bolster its assailed weaker positions, thus rendering its former strong positions more vulnerable. My experience with the zoning board illustrates that a similar approach succeeds in negotiations. The key official was initially firm in his opposition to my client's request, but he capitulated once his weakness—his great fear of multi-family unit development in the area—was exposed and assailed.

Timing is everything. The key question to ask yourself is: When will use of my power have the greatest impact, the greatest influence on motivating my opponent towards my negotiating objectives? In both the Carnegie and rezoning examples, the answer was *before* actual commencement of negotiation. In the antique-car example, power was used *after* negotiations had begun, once the owner discovered the buyer possessed a strong desire for the car and would be fearful of losing it to someone else.

R. J. Reynolds's timing was also effective in his confrontation with James Duke over the tobacco takeover. Suddenly confronted with an ultimatum, Reynolds could have delayed his response by telling Duke he had to think the matter over. Such a delay, however, would have allowed the threat, which Reynolds knew Duke was perfectly capable of carrying out, to play on Reynolds's mind and, thus, grow. All sorts of painful visions of a lost business, bankruptcy, and family travails would have undoubtedly danced in Reynolds's consciousness. Wisely, Reynolds decided to strike back immediately. Perhaps he responded forcefully and confidently with a threat of his own because he was angry and bent on revenge. Whatever the reason, his own ultimatum put the necessary fear in Duke to pay the three million dollars Reynolds was after.

The common theme in all these stories is that fear is a tremendous motivator. We all harbor fears that play an important role in the way we conduct our lives. Very few of us are fearless.

LET YOUR POWER SHOW

Picture this unusual scenario. A man dressed as a circus clown walks into a bank. Smiling broadly, he happily works his way to a teller, passing out candy to the bank's customers as he goes. With a laugh, he advises the teller that it's a stickup. Obviously, the teller will be a little anxious but will probably wonder whether the whole thing is some sort of promotion or even a prank. Clowns are associated with laughter; bank robbery is not. The clown has, thus, not properly conveyed the seriousness of his demands. But suppose the clown then whips out a sawed-off shotgun from under his loosely fitting costume. The mere sight of the gun will get his message home. The teller will undoubtedly be gripped with great fear. By suddenly revealing the gun, the clown has made the teller aware of the true extent of his power.

In the everyday world of negotiations, you must fully appraise your opponents of the true extent of your power. In this instance, what your opponents don't know, won't hurt them. Not heeding this principle is a major cause of failure in negotiation. Incredibly, many negotiators commit this mistake deliberately, deciding to hold knowledge of their power "in reserve" for possible use later should the situation demand.

Knowledge of your negotiating power should never be held in reserve. You may, as a matter of strategy, withhold *use* of your power; but even if you do that, your opponent must be made completely aware of the extent of the power that you could choose to exercise. Once the bank-robbing clown produced the shotgun, the teller immediately possessed complete knowledge of the clown's power, which would motivate the teller to pass over the cash. The clown would then not have to use his power, namely, shooting the shotgun.

The distinction, then, is between *knowledge* of power and *use* of power. Never withhold knowledge of your power. But use your power only at what you determine are the strategic times in the negotiation.

The Lawyer's Malady

Lawyers are particularly prone to holding knowledge of their power in reserve, especially in relation to litigation. Rather than disclose in settlement negotiations the true extent of their power, they opt to hold key portions back for use at the trial in the event no settlement is reached. It is a bad tactic.

The beginning of a trial signifies the failure of negotiations, which may have been the result of a lawyer not disclosing power in a timely and, therefore, effective manner. Failure is, thus, programmed into the strategy of holding knowledge of power in reserve. Moreover, the vast majority of lawsuits are settled out of court, many immediately before commencement of the trial. Hence, any tactic that hinders settlement fails to recognize statistical probability. In fact, as trial time approaches, pressure for settlement mounts; the uncertainty of jury trials in particular forces the hand of many negotiators. Thus, delay in imparting knowledge of negotiating power, without good strategic reason, is often power lost.

The safest and best policy is to make certain your opponent is fully aware of the true extent of your negotiating power. This will provide you with greater assurance that your power will play an important role in the final negotiation outcome, as, indeed, it should.

The Power of Repetition

Anything repeated often enough will be believed. If the proposition that the world as it is now known will come to an end in ten years is repeated often enough and in a variety of ways—by word of mouth, in newspapers, on television, and so on—a significant number of people will come to believe that the event will actually occur and even make preparations for it. Although not everyone will believe everything (the impending end of the world, for instance), everyone does tend to believe what is constantly repeated. Repetition is, thus, a potent force and, hence, a very powerful negotiating technique. The Russians, for example, are acutely aware of the value in negotiation of endless repetition, taking every opportunity to iterate then reiterate key points they want to emphasize.

It is vitally important for you not only to apprise your opponent of the true extent of your power in a timely manner, but to make sure that understanding is maintained throughout the *entire* negotiation. Awareness may dim with the passage of time during a long negotiation, emotions may drive it out, and people can simply forget. Once the awareness is gone from your opponent's mind, your power has diminished. Skillfully repeating during the course of the negotiation the true extent of your power is, therefore, a necessity—both to keep it in the forefront of your opponent's mind and to magnify its impact.

To illustrate, I was faced with a negotiation that promised to extend over a long period of time because of the complex issues involved. I was possessed of certain facts that provided considerable support to my case and, thus, gave me a great deal of negotiating power. I wanted to commence the first session by revealing those facts and so seize the offense early in the proceedings. (An old but wise adage applicable to negotiating holds that "a bungling attack is better than the most skillful defense." Offense scores points, and it's points that win the game.) I had to make certain, however, that using my facts early would not mean that they would lose their impact as the negotiations dragged on. Repetition became the vehicle I rode to victory. I simply reiterated the key supporting facts at every opportunity, both orally and in written documents, blending them into my entire presentation until they were indelibly etched in my opponent's mind.

This repetition was critical to the successful outcome of the negotiation. It allowed what constituted my negotiating power to have the greatest possible impact. Using your power in a timely manner, thus, doesn't mean you only get to use it once. Keep knowledge of your power always in the forefront of your opponent's mind for the best results.

Variety Is the Spice of Repetition

Remember that the human brain can receive information only through one of more of the five senses: sight, hearing, touch, taste, and smell. The two most important and most widely used are sight and hearing. If you orally advise your opponent of the extent of your negotiating power, you have adopted one means of reaching your opponent's mind. If you combine your oral approach with, for example, the submission of written data, you have magnified your effectiveness through use of variety in repetition.

When I was negotiating the value of a large parcel of real estate, I had an extensive appraisal of the property made. The appraisal was put in writing and included elaborate color pictures. I could have orally related my thoughts on the value of the property and reinforced my presentation with the written proposal. That would have effectively repeated the message for my opponent through two media, sight and hearing. But to magnify the impact further, I suggested a drive out to the property so that my opponent and I could look at it together. He agreed.

When we arrived, I gave him a copy of the appraisal. Right there on the scene we

1. viewed the actual property (which reached my opponent through his sense of sight),

2. reviewed key portions of the appraisal (sense of sight), and

3. discussed how certain elements in the appraisal related to the actual site (thus reaching him through his sense of hearing).

Thus, I was able to literally bombard my opponent with repetition of the merits of my cause through his senses of sight and hearing. If I had been limited to oral arguments, the constant reiteration of salient points would have been far less effective. My opponent, for instance, might have construed my obvious repetition as a sign of weakness or decided that I was trying to hide elements detrimental to my position.

Using repetition effectively, then, does not mean simply reiterating the same line over and over again like a broken record. On the contrary, you must vary your approach by employing more than one medium to get information to your opponent. Try to reach your opponent's mind through as many of the five senses as possible, concentrating on sight and hearing, just as I did in the foregoing real estate negotiation.

CHAPTER 4

Never Get Picked Off Base

Setting and Maintaining Primary and Secondary Bases for Each Negotiating Session

Perfection is attained by slow degrees; it requires the hand of time.

Voltaire

Take time to consider and then decide quickly.

Rothschild

The proper study of mankind is man.

Pope

During the course of a negotiation that ran continuously for seven to eight hours, one of the critical issues discussed revolved around a clause in a contract that granted my client the option to repurchase a certain asset after a period of years had elapsed. Counsel for the other side wanted that provision out of the agreement because his client was very reluctant to let go of an asset that he felt would be quite profitable somewhere down the road. My client, on the other hand, was just as adamant that the option provision remain because it was central to his future planning.

I, therefore, remained firm in defense of my client's position. My opponent objected strenuously, declaring that the valuation formula in the option clause did not take into consideration any goodwill after the expiration period had elapsed.

I said, "Let's add it in."

He then altered his tactics by contending that the formula did not specify the exact number of years prior to the option date that must be considered in arriving at the value of the asset.

I said, "Let's add it in."

He then countered that the language of the proposition did not provide that all relevant valuation factors be considered in arriving at the buy-back price.

I said, "Let's add it in."

He agreed.

PRIMARY AND SECONDARY BASES

Virtually every negotiable issue has what can be called a "primary base" and one or more "secondary bases." Your ultimate objective for each issue is your primary base. Positive factors that support the primary base are the secondary bases.

As the language suggests, the concept can be illustrated in baseball terms. The primary base/objective of every time at bat (negotiating issue) is to score a run. To do that, you must touch the (secondary) bases: first, second, third, and home plate. Failure to touch these bases (you're out!) means failure to reach your goal (no score). This happens a lot in the negotiation game. In negotiations, you must not only keep your mind on scoring, you must also concentrate on touching the bases.

The Primary Base

In the option-contract example that opened the chapter, my opponent lost sight of his primary base. His goal should have been to delete the buy-back clause from the agreement; my objective on that issue was to keep it in. If I would have allowed my primary base to escape from the forefront of my thoughts, I might have negotiated a key provision away and, thus, failed my client.

All the points raised by my opponent, and acceded to by me, were valuation factors normally considered when arriving at the value of an asset like the one in question. Adding them to the contract clause did not, therefore, detract even the slightest from my primary base. Because I readily agreed to each of them without hesitation, my opponent became flustered and confused— and the option provision remained in the contract.

Another Primary Base Illustration

I represented a party interested in acquiring a large tract of land. One of the issues concerned the manner in which the property would be purchased. My client's ultimate goal, or primary base, was to pay as little as possible over the first ten years. My client felt it would take that long for growth to catch up to the property and, therefore, make it ripe for development. In addition, my client wanted the bulk of any payments over that ten-year period to constitute interest rather than principal so that the payments would enjoy certain tax benefits, which would further reduce the true cost of acquiring the land.

The sellers, on the other hand, wanted to get as much as possible of the purchase price paid immediately and, further, wanted the balance paid over a relatively short period of time. They were heirs to an estate and were desirous of getting as much money as soon as they could. Knowledge of their primary base, of course, swung considerable negotiating power to our side. We readily agreed to add a little to the purchase price and to increase the interest rate on the balance as long as the sellers agreed to only a 20 percent down payment and to allow my client a 30-year amortization of the unpaid balance with the full unpaid balance payable in ten years.[*]

Amortizing the unpaid balance over a 30-year period, thus, meant that virtually all of my client's annual payments would constitute interest rather than principal. The tax benefits gained would more than offset the increased purchase price and interest rate. Those conditions, plus the ten-year payoff, met my client's ultimate objective for this issue; we had achieved the primary base. The sellers, on the other hand, lost sight of their primary objective. They had wanted as much money as possible up front and the rest soon after. The increased purchase price and interest rate distracted them. As it turned out, they had to wait a full ten years for the bulk of the purchase price. When that time arrived, market value of the land had, as my client anticipated, increased significantly. My client, therefore, reaped substantial

---

[*]A 30-year amortization would result in unpaid-balance payments that were *calculated* over a 30-year period.

benefits, because I kept a steady eye on my client's primary base while negotiating that issue.

HOW TO KEEP THE PRIMARY BASE FROM GETTING LOST

Essentially, negotiators fail to attain an objective, the primary base, for two reasons. Surprisingly, one common cause is failure to even set a primary base on each negotiable issue. Often, negotiators will begin discussions with only a general goal in mind for the final outcome of the entire negotiation but with no specific objectives on each issue to be negotiated. That's not unlike ignoring the stairs and attempting to leap right to the top of the building—Ok for Superman but not for the rest of us. We mortals would do better to emulate the late, legendary billionaire Howard Hughes rather than "The Man of Steel."

The Lesson of Howard Hughes

Howard Hughes identified primary bases (specific objectives) for each issue in any negotiation and insisted that whoever was handling negotiations for him attain those primary bases. As you would expect, many of the contracts Hughes entered into involved large sums of money and numerous complex issues. Hughes would instruct his representative as to which matters absolutely had to be resolved favorably. For instance, in a negotiation for the purchase of new airplanes, Hughes would identify two aspects critical to him: price and delivery date. He needed to establish the latter to his satisfaction in order to calculate when his new planes could be put into service and so generate income. Hughes, thus, would instruct his negotiators to stand firm on price and delivery date and to make concessions, if they had to be made, on issues he considered less important, such as terms of payment and nonmaterial airplane specifications that Hughes felt would not detract from his intended use of the planes.

Keep Your Eye on the (Primary) Base

You won't get to where you want to go if you lose sight of your destination. Even if you set clear primary objectives for each issue, you won't reach them if you are distracted during the normal give and take of negotiations. Recall what happened to the property sellers when the temptations of an increased purchase price and interest rate on the unpaid balance dangled before them. Their vision of receiving more money overrode or blocked out their primary objective of getting as much for the property as possible, as early as possible.

Losing sight of one's primary base is frequently caused by the pressures of negotiation. The ability to think and act coolly under pressure is essential to success in negotiation, but it comes only from experience. Some negotiators make mistakes; *learn* from their mistakes, and go on to develop greater skills. Others just continue to make the same mistakes time after time. They are simply unable to adjust to dealing with the pressures. These people are easy to spot; they are usually loaded with bad negotiating habits such as:

1. Smoking so profusely during the actual negotiations that the procedure of lighting up, puffing, discarding ashes, and so forth, interferes with their concentration. Even heavily addicted smokers tend to smoke more under the pressure.

2. Drinking coffee or other beverages excessively. On occasion, this can become so pronounced that the

individual must take frequent breaks for bladder relief, often during critical times during the negotiation.

3. Constantly interrupting the discussion without actually having heard what has been said. By responding in this way, the interrupting party cannot discover all that's on the opponent's mind, thus prohibiting the most effective application of the best available strategies and tactics.

One attorney I negotiated against had such a pronounced blinking habit when the negotiations became intense that it appeared as though he were about to come apart. The pressure was simply too much for him. He was fully aware of his excessive blinking but was powerless to stop it. He was so distracted that his thinking became fuzzy, and he lost concentration on his primary base on each negotiating issue. It was truly regrettable.

Skilled negotiators, of course, are alert to an opponent's behavior under the mental rigors of negotiation. If a weakness is evident, they deliberately turn up the pressure a notch or two in hopes of dislodging the unraveling individual's concentration from the primary base, and even from the secondary bases. Such ploys underscore the fact that negotiation is a conflict between minds. To win, you must cultivate the ability to remain cool and calm, to think clearly, when the pressure is intense.

Here are two "tricks" that will help you cope:

1. *Don't Hesitate to Take a "Pause that Refreshes"*

If at any point during a negotiating session you feel you are beginning to yield to the pressure, immediately seek a recess. Do so even when the negotiation is informal, such as one conducted over the telephone. Just suggest you would like to think the matter over and promise to return soon to the discussions. During the respite, carefully analyze your position, with particular emphasis on whether you are straying from any of your primary bases. If you find you have lost sight of your objectives, then take steps to get back on track when the session resumes. Over a period of time, this process will help train you to deal effectively with the pressures inherent in virtually any negotiation of consequence.

2. *Watch What and How Much You Eat*

Diet, too, is an important element in effectively dealing with negotiation pressures. Stay away from stimulants like caffeine and sugar, as well as from other harmful substances like alcohol, especially immediately prior to and during the actual discussions. Drugs, of course, should be avoided at all times.

Eat lightly before each negotiating session. Heavy food dulls the thinking process and should be refused if offered by a crafty opponent looking for an edge. Sound farfetched? I was, in fact, involved in a situation in which food was used as a weapon. In that instance, negotiations were quite complex, and several parties participated. The host for the discussions always insisted that talks be held in his company's conference room, commencing near lunch hour. After about an hour, we would break for a catered lunch, which consisted of huge, delicious-looking sandwiches. Most of the participants filled up on the good food, but our host refrained, and so did I. Neither one of us wanted to blunt our mental faculties. We remained alert, while the others who had eaten their fill struggled to keep their eyes open.

Cicero, the great Roman orator, politician, and philosopher, put it best: "We cannot employ the mind to advantage when we are filled with excessive food and drink."

SECONDARY BASES

Secondary bases are those *positive* factors that are related to the issue being discussed and that support the primary base. They must be touched in order to reach the primary objectives of each negotiating issue.

The following everyday situation illustrates the concept clearly. Assume you are in need a quart of oil for your car. That is your primary base. The positive factors in your favor, that is, the secondary bases, are (1) you have a car with room for a quart of oil; (2) you have money to pay for the quart of oil; and (3) besides the one you are at now, there is a gas station across the street or down the block (there always is) that would welcome your business. The transaction might proceed as follows:

"I'll take a quart of your best oil, please," you say to the station owner.

The station owner is enterprising and therefore sets out to negotiate a larger sale. "Oil changes are on special today if you fill up with our premium gas. It's a real savings, but the offer ends today." (Specials always seem to expire in a very short time.) The deadline makes you anxious and thus increases the station owner's negotiating power.

"I don't have that much time," you reply.

"Have you out of here in five minutes."

"Well, I appreciate it, but I don't have that much cash."

"Your credit card's good." (Everybody has one or more of those.)

The dialogue continues until you submit and buy a complete oil change and a full tank of premium gas, which means, of course, that you lost sight of your primary base—to simply get a quart of oil. And the secondary bases? To use them, you need only to have said: "All my car needs is one quart of your best oil. How much is it?" Reaching for your cash and glancing quickly but obviously across the street or down the block toward the competition would have gotten you the quart of oil forthwith. You would, thus, have reached your primary base.

Using Secondary Bases in Negotiation

In one of my negotiations with the Internal Revenue Service, the central issue involved arriving at the fair market value of more than 115,000 shares of common stock of a company listed on the New York Stock Exchange. Call the company the ABC Corporation. On the date that value was to be determined, market price of the ABC stock was slightly more than $100 a share, for a total, gross value of over $11.5 million. I contended, however, that the valuation should be significantly less because of the large number of shares. The theory was that flooding the market with more than 115,000 shares would depress prices well below the currently listed $100 per share. (Valuation reduction, such as this, resulting from transactions involving a large number of shares is called "blockage" or "material blockage.")

My primary base for this negotiation issue was, of course, to obtain as large a per-share reduction as possible for my client. My specific goal was $5 a share, any reduction greater than that would, I felt, be a bonus.

I faced several roadblocks to gaining my objective. One was the IRS's reluctance to grant material blockage discounts or, for that matter, any discounts. Material blockage discounts would mean a lower valuation of the ABC stock, which would mean lower taxes for my client, since the tax rate was applied to the value of the stock. Thus, the IRS would not be inclined to favor a discount from the $100 market price unless the issue was clearcut for my client, which it was not. In fact, blockage was strictly a judgment issue. It would, therefore, take considerable effort to win the government over to my position.

Another negative factor was ABC's strong reputation. Not many stockholders wanted to sell. As a result, fewer than 2,000 shares of the company were traded on an average day. The down side—what made this a negative factor for me, and, thus, a positive factor for my opponent, the IRS—was that should a large number of shares become available, there would be ready buyers, meaning prices might not be depressed as much as I was contending.

There were other negative factors that would also hinder me from reaching my goal of a $5-a-share reduction in valuation. What I needed for my secondary bases, however, were positive factors that supported my primary base. I concentrated on four items.

1. The number of shares being valued (over 115,000) represented a sizable block of stock, in and of itself. (Even if very friendly, a 115,000 pound gorilla sits any where he wants.)

2. Less than 2,000 shares a day were being traded on average.

3. Of the some 11 million shares authorized and issued by the company to the public, approximately 80 percent, or 8.8 million, was not actively traded on the market because it was either held in trust or held by people who preferred to keep the stock for long-term investment. Thus, my client's more than 115,000 shares became an even larger percentage of the 2.2 million remaining shares *available for trading*. (In financial circles, the number of shares actually available for trading in the market is commonly referred to as *float*.)

4. With a relatively narrow or small float, a block of

shares in excess of 115,000 very likely would have a depressing impact on the market price of the stock.

You've probably noticed that secondary bases are a lot like political debates: how they are evaluated, positive or negative, depends on the "spin," or interpretation, put on them. I had to stress the relative magnitudes of the numbers themselves, especially those in items 2 and 4, to put a positive spin on these bases. The IRS, on the other hand, would focus, as already mentioned, on the reason behind the low number of transactions and the large number of shares held for long-term investment: namely, that the company had a strong reputation.

Because of the money involved, negotiations on this issue extended over a lengthy period. Each dollar reduction in per-share value meant a reduction in the overall value of the stock of over $115,000, which, in turn, meant my client's tax bill would be significantly lower. At each negotiating session, as circumstances warranted, I stressed my secondary bases. Without them, my chances of achieving the primary base of a $5 reduction were nil. Finally, the IRS agreed to allow a valuation reduction of $7.50 per share (a gross valuation reduction of over $860,000). I had exceeded my primary base and won a very tidy tax saving for my client.

WHY SECONDARY BASES ARE LOST

Negotiators lose sight of secondary bases for the same reasons they lose slight of primary bases—either they fail to set secondary bases on each negotiable issue or they are distracted by the pressure generated during the heat of battle. The latter cause is common. In fact, failure to maintain secondary bases is directly proportional to the complexity of the negotiations and the number of issues involved.

The problem is compounded by the number of secondary bases. Since any one primary base might have numerous positive factors in support, the negotiator first must isolate and list these secondary bases. Those bases must then be maintained and used throughout the entire course of discussions, as the circumstances warrant, when the pressure is on to perform. This entails conditioning the mind to avoid the mental blocks that are a frequent occurrence in negotiations, particularly when the issues are numerous and complex and the give and take becomes heated and emotional. It also means conditioning the mind to easily, quickly, and effectively jump from issue to issue without losing sight of the secondary bases for each issue under discussion. Experienced negotiators might deliberately skip from one issue to another and back again to confuse and muddle their opponent's thinking. Russian negotiators, in fact, are especially adept at unexpectedly shifting from issue to issue in order to create confusion and chaos.

THE ILICH SECONDARY-BASE SYSTEM

Whether you are faced with Russians or crafty Americans across the negotiating table, I've perfected a system that will materially help you keep your bases in alignment and in sight no matter how difficult and drawnout the negotiations.

First, on paper, list each secondary base for each negotiable issue. Then commit every item to memory. As a final check, just before entering a negotiating session, quickly scan your written lists to be certain that every base is firmly in the forefront of your mind. This list-and-check system will allow you to pull your secondary bases from your memory easily and to use them during discussions effectively as you see fit. This ability has a depressing impact on opponents, especially if they have been trying to confuse you by leaping from issue to issue. There is literally nowhere they can go that you cannot follow.

The Stock Valuation Example Revisited

To illustrate the Ilich Secondary Base System, let's revisit the stock valuation example. Before embarking on any discussion of the issue, I composed a written list of secondary bases. It looked like this:

SECONDARY BASES—
115,000-PLUS SHARES ABC CORPORATION

1. 115,000+ shares is a sizable block.

2. Shares of ABC Corporation actually traded at or near valuation date is less than 2,000 daily.

3. 80 percent of shares issued, or some 8,800,000 shares is not actively traded on the market.

4. Such a small float means 115,000+, if sold, would have depressing market impact.

Since I had previously determined each of my secondary bases and knew each thoroughly and in detail, this condensed list was sufficient for review and reference. Thus, it was easy for me to use the bases during the actual negotiation. I could, for example, point out when appropriate that such a small float meant that 115,000 shares, even if sold over a reasonable period of time, would substantially depress the market price well below $100 per share (secondary base 4), especially since fewer than 2,000 shares of ABC Corporation were traded daily (secondary base 2), and, as a consequence, the market price would probably fall to $90 to $92. As related, my approach was highly effective.

FINDING NEW SECONDARY BASES DURING NEGOTIATION

By now, you've no doubt noticed that successful negotiation is a mix of preparation and flexibility. Those twin principles apply to the use of secondary bases as well. As just discussed, careful preparation helps you to determine the right secondary bases ahead of time and to use them when appropriate. But you must also be sufficiently flexible to take advantage of secondary bases that might emerge as the negotiation progresses. Be alert to disclosures by opponents that can be turned to your advantage. These can be particularly powerful because you can attribute the information to your opponent and win substantial concessions as a result.

A negotiation in which I represented the prospective purchaser of a business illustrates well the value of discovered secondary bases. The balance sheet of the business in question revealed substantial debt in the form of loans payable. The seller wanted my client to assume the debt. We felt that would make the price of the acquisition too much to pay. The break in this seeming impasse came during casual conversation with the seller/owner. He began reminiscing about how close he was to the business, how he had built it up from nothing, and, therefore, how he had mixed emotions about selling. He revealed that he paid off, from his personal account, much of the bank debt as it came due during the early, lean years when the business was unable to generate sufficient cash flow to do so.

That disclosure immediately raised the question of how much of the balance-sheet debt represented money the business owed the owner. An investigation revealed that the bulk of it was. This knowledge, of course, presented us with an excellent opportunity to reduce the overall cost of acquiring the business. We could propose either simply eliminating all or a considerable portion of the personal debt owed by the business to the seller/ owner, or we could suggest reducing the sales price by all or part of that debt. The personal debt owed by the business to the seller thus became a positive factor in attaining my client's primary objective and, therefore, emerged as one of my secondary bases in the negotiation.

Besides remaining constantly alert to such good fortune as the inadvertent disclosure, you can also intentionally probe your opponent, even during informal gab sessions, for information that may prove useful. One excellent method is simply to ask questions. It is truly amazing how readily people answer questions about themselves and their interests. Not infrequently, they reveal something you can use. People respond to questions as though duty bound to do so; but there is an art in the asking.

General Versus Specific Questions

It is important to understand the differences between general and specific questions and how to use them. General questions are excellent for probing and best used during the early stages of a negotiation when there is a legitimate reason for asking. Used early, they are excellent tools for soliciting information that can add to your secondary bases. That's how, in the previously related example, I was able to learn of the debt the business owed to the seller. When he began reminiscing, I inquired whether it had been difficult for him to obtain financing. He said it was, indeed, tough and, once he got financing, he had to pay off the lender himself each time a portion of the loan came due in order to maintain a good credit rating. I was able to probe with general questions (and invite damaging disclosures) because it was the appropriate time to ask. Asking general questions when the negotiation is well under way, however, may not only discredit your preparation and ability, but also make your opponent suspicious of your motives. The seller may not have been so open later in the negotiations.

Specific questions, on the other hand, are useful at any stage of the negotiation, although more so in the later stages when you are more apt to know precisely what you are after. Be advised, however, that sharp and experienced opponents may recognize your attempt to gain useful information and will either decline to respond or will answer in a way calculated to frustrate your purposes. They may even try to mislead you. Furthermore, knowing they have thwarted you may give your opponents a psychological victory, boost their confidence, and make them tougher negotiators. Accordingly, ask specific questions with great discretion and only when you have definitely determined that the need for and the chances of getting information outweigh the risk of tipping off your opponents.

Still, you may on occasion find yourself with few or even no secondary bases of consequence on a particular issue. With all the cards stacked against you, do not hesitate to venture both general and specific questions—*provided that asking does not discredit you on other, more important, issues that must be negotiated.* Jeopardizing critical issues to gain information to use as secondary bases on lesser ones is folly and should be avoided.

CHAPTER 5

Tit for Tat

How to Make Sure That You Keep the Negotiation Equalized

Colors fade, temples crumble, empires fall, but wise words endure.

Thorndike

Nine-tenths of wisdom is being wise in time.

Theodore Roosevelt

To carry your cargo and make your port is the point. Pay as little attention to discouragement as possible.

Babcock

There is an old saying that a person persuaded against his will is of the same opinion still. That adage goes to the heart of the negotiation concept of equalization. To understand what equalization is and appreciate its importance, consider the following simple example.

KEEPING THE SALE OF A YACHT ON EVEN KEEL

Suppose a boat enthusiast wants to purchase a yacht that happens to be 20 years old. She points out the age of the vessel, seeking, of course, a lower purchase price. That's a valid argument; a 20-year-old boat is certainly worth much less than a new craft of the same model and size. If the seller fails to advance a position of equal weight and validity to match the buyer's argument, he will not get a top price for the yacht.

Why? Because once the buyer advances the argument that the age of the yacht warrants a lower price, she will remain mentally fixed on that position so long as the seller fails to present a legitimate response that will *in the buyer's mind* equalize, or balance, her contention about the yacht's age and value. Let me reemphasize the key words: *in the buyer's mind*. It does no good for the seller to advance a position that satisfies only him that he has made a satisfactory counter. The *buyer must be convinced* that the seller's response answers the argument fully.

The burden is on both negotiating parties to be certain that the arguments and positions they advance fully satisfy *each other's* sense of equality, not just their own.

At this stage of the negotiation, the weight of the argument is clearly in the buyer's favor. The seller is hopelessly up in the air and must do something to at least balance the scales if he is to get anything approaching his price for the yacht. This situation is depicted graphically, using a balance-beam scale, in Figure 1.

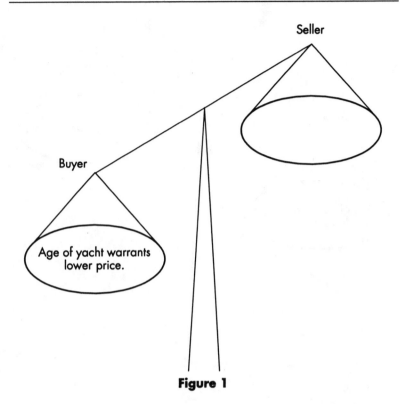

Figure 1

Assume the seller counters with the assertion that age doesn't necessarily mean that a quality yacht, like his, is worth less than a new model. Unfortunately for the seller, that position is probably too weak to change the mind of the buyer about age and the price of yachts. Thus, the seller would still not have equalized the arguments, as depicted in Figure 2.

In order to achieve equalization, the seller must advance a position of *substance* that is *relevant* to the buyer's argument. Although the seller's argument is relevant because it deals with the age issue, it is not of substance unless he can produce some supportive facts. A recent sale of a yacht of comparable age and model at a comparable price, for example, would constitute such factual support and, thus, would equal the weight of the buyer's argument.

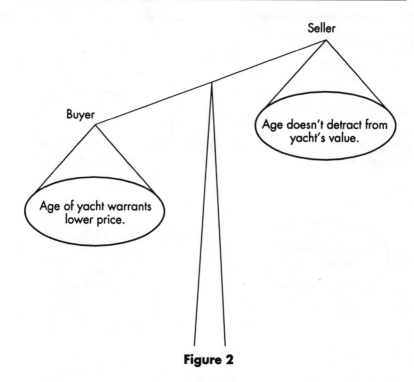

Buyer

Age of yacht warrants
lower price.

Seller

Age doesn't detract from
yacht's value.

Figure 2

Suppose that such evidence of the irrelevance of age is not available. The seller might next claim that over its 20 years, the yacht has been fully tried and tested under all kinds of sailing conditions, including heavy, stormy seas. He would then advance a second position—that the buyer could, therefore, place greater reliability on his yacht than on a new, unproven one.

That would be a novel and perhaps valid argument, but is it sufficient to change the mind of the buyer and convince her that the age of the yacht does not warrant a lower price? Probably not, unless the seller can offer some credible proof that will satisfy her. Thus, at this stage of the negotiation, the balance scale would be tipped still in favor of the buyer, as shown in Figure 3.

Remaining persistent, as a negotiator must, the seller puts forth a third argument—that the yacht was com-

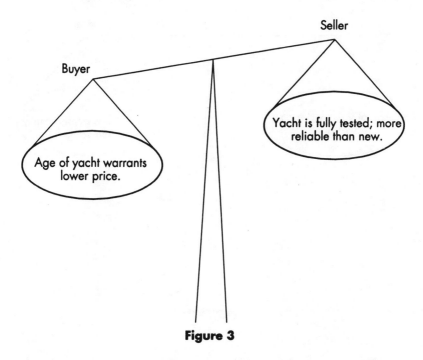

Figure 3

pletely remodeled a year ago, bringing it up to the standards of a new craft. That position is one of substance and is directly relevant to the buyer's age contention. It would, therefore, clearly equalize the buyer's position, assuming the seller's assertion was accurate and could be proven. The seller would be under obligation, if req uired by the buyer, to document the full extent of the remodeling and to disclose who did the job, since the skill of the craftsman would have an important bearing on the quality of the remodeling.

Now the seller has put forth an argument equal *in the buyer's mind* to the buyer's position that the age of the yacht warrants a lower price and has, thus, completely equalized the negotiation, as shown in Figure 4. The sellers chances of obtaining a top price for the yach have been substantially enhanced.

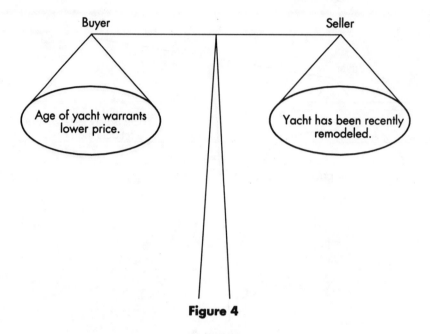

Figure 4

But the seller decides to add more weight to his side of the scale. He declares that the yacht was formerly owned by a celebrity. This situation makes the vessel more desirable and more valuable, especially if the celebrity is very famous. Objects owned by famous people usually possess an intrinsic value that traditionally has commanded a higher sales price. Indeed, the celebrity aspect alone can increase the price of an object in relation to its true value well beyond all bounds of reason.

By playing the celebrity card, the seller has tipped the balance in his favor and is now in control of the negotiation. The respective positions of the parties are depicted, one last time, in Figure 5.

The burden has now clearly shifted to the buyer to equalize the negotiation. She will try to advance positions that will fully satisfy the seller in his own mind that the past celebrity ownership does not warrant a higher selling price. If she fails, she will have to pay top dollar to acquire the yacht.

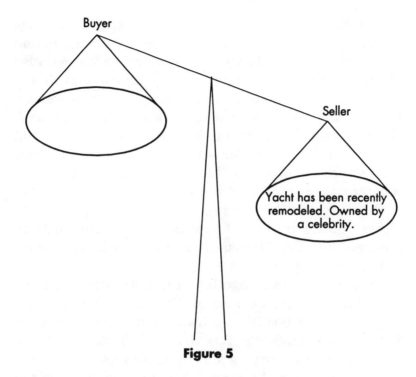

Figure 5

That in simple form is how the equalization process works in negotiation. The next illustrative case offers a few more complications.

EQUALIZING A REAL ESTATE DEAL

The negotiation involves a parcel of land located on a prime spot for an office park. The property is basically level, so no expensive grading will be necessary. It is near a large shopping mall and all forms of transportation, including an interstate highway and the area's major airport. Another buyer is interested in the property, and the seller has already turned down an offer of $500,000, seeking, instead, $600,000.

But the site does have drawbacks. Tests reveal subsoil problems that will increase the cost of laying a foundation. Zoning regulations limit the height of buildings that can be constructed on the property. Entrance to and exit from the property are somewhat restricted because of the nearness of curb cuts to a busy intersection. Sewer and water lines are 300 feet from the property boundary, so there will be extra costs to hook into these services. The $500,000 offer from a different potential buyer that was rejected by the seller was for 20 percent down and the balance payable over five years. The present buyer is willing to pay $500,000 in cash. He has learned from a reliable source that the seller can offset any profit from a sale (for tax purposes) against losses incurred from previous, unrelated transactions; thus, she has an incentive for making the deal.

Each side in this negotiation has six good positions that, if advanced in a wise and timely fashion, should fully offset the positions advanced by the other side. Seldom does such equality occur. In fact, it is more common for one party's good negotiating positions to far outweigh those of the other. This does not necessarily mean, however, that the stronger side will prevail in the negotiation. Holding the cards is one thing, playing them deftly is entirely another. The skill and experience of the negotiators will ultimately determine the outcome.

For purposes of this illustration, assume the seller and buyer have comparable experience and skills as negotiators. The focus will then be on how equally good positions are played out. The negotiating positions of both parties are summarized in the lists below.

Positions Favorable to Seller

1. Property is prime for office park.
2. Property is level and so no expensive grading is needed.
3. Complete shopping facilities are near the site.
4. Property is near all forms of transportation.

5. Another buyer is interested in the property.

6. Seller turned down a $500,000 offer from another buyer.

Positions Favorable to Buyer

1. Soil tests indicate increased costs of constructing foundation.

2. Zoning restrictions limit the height of buildings.

3. Entrance to and exit from the property are restricted by curb cuts.

4. Additional costs are necessary to bring sewer and water 300 feet to the property.

5. Offer already rejected was in time payments, not cash.

6. Seller would like to deal in order to offset gains against losses from other transactions.

When negotiations commence, the seller leads by asserting that the property is prime for an office park and that she has already rejected a $500,000 offer (positions 1 and 6, respectively). To achieve equalization, the buyer must counter with positions of substance that are relevant to the seller's positions. The buyer has plenty of ammunition to do that. He can respond, for example, that soil tests indicate that constructing the foundations will cost more than usual (buyer's position 1), zoning regulations restrict the height of buildings (position 2), and ingress and egress to and from the property are also restricted (position 3). These positions are not only substantial, they are relevant because they reflect adversely on the quality of the location (not so "prime" afterall) for an office park.

Equalizing the seller's position of an already spurned offer also should be fairly easy. Again, the criteria are that the advanced positions must be of substance and must be relevant to the opposition's positions. If, for example, the buyer countered with his position 4 on the costs of sewer and water service, he would not have equalized the $500,000 offer, even though that issue is substantial, because it is not directly relevant and, furthermore, not of sufficient substance to balance the scale. Many negotiators fail to attain equalization quickly and effectively because they have difficulty selecting from all the options available the precise position that will equalize what their opponents have advanced. This problem is magnified when the negotiation involves a number of complex issues and the sessions run over a long period of time.

In our example, the buyer does have a response to the previously rejected $500,000 offer that is both relevant and sufficiently substantial. He can point out that the first offer was for 20 percent down with the balance over five years; he, on the other hand, will pay cash. This counter evokes buyer positions 5 and 6 because the buyer knows the seller would like to unload the property to offset losses on other transactions. The buyer has, thus, met his need to equalize the seller's opening position.

The burden is always on the responding party. Failure to assume that burden means failure to attain negotiating objectives. The principle applies to both buyers and sellers, of course, as illustrated by the continuing negotiations.

In round two, having achieved equalization, the buyer advances position 4 that he will incur additional expense to bring sewer and water to the property. That's a raw, basic, dollars-and-cents argument. In essence, the buyer is saying the property is not worth as much because of the distance to water and sewer connections. To equalized that position, the seller should counter with another dollar-and-cents argument. At her disposal is her position 2, that the property is basically level and will not require any expensive grading. This responds directly to the buyer's sewer-and-water argument and is both relevant and substantial; it addresses his out-of-pocket concerns with an element of equal magnitude.

In contrast, this would not be an appropriate time to mention the proximity of the property to the shopping center. That's a position of substance but not directly relevant to the sewer and water issue raised by the buyer. Nor would a counter declaring the existence of another buyer be relevant here. That position may create fear of losing the property to a competitor in the buyer and so afford the seller negotiating power, but it is not strictly responsive to the buyer's position. However, once equalization is reached again with the seller's level-ground position, she might gain an advantage by combining that response with the disclosure of another potential purchaser. The scale would then be tilted in her favor, and the burden would be on the buyer to advance another position to bring the negotiation back to a condition of equalization.

This jockeying back and forth is typical in most negotiations. The equalization scale moves up and down many times during a normal session. And, as has been shown, the craft of equalizing an opponent's position requires skill and experience.

THE HAZARDS OF EQUALIZATION

Napoleon once observed that in affairs of magnitude everything invariably turns upon a trifle. His insight is particularly applicable to equalization because failure to equalize even one solid argument advanced by an opponent can spell failure for the negotiator. And the greater the number of issues to be negotiated and the greater their complexity, the more difficult it becomes to attain equalization. A comparative analysis of the yacht and real estate examples should make that plain: as the number and complexity of choices (of positions) increases, so does the task of selection. Further, in complex negotiations, the need for equalization arises constantly. Difficulties, thus, increase exponentially.

In addition, negotiators often must attain equalization during the heat of discussions when the pressures are considerable and one's ability to think and act clearly and coolly is inhibited. Also, equalizing the opposing party's position is largely a matter of proper timing. Negotiators must strike while the iron is hot; they do not have the luxury of retreating from the fray to reflect on ways and means. By that time, an important advantage may have been irretrievably lost.

The combination of the abundance of complex issues, the numerous positions from which to choose a response to an opponent, the pressures of heated debate, and the critical need for good timing can make the achievement of equalization throughout the negotiation quite difficult indeed. Failure brings disaster, but success is possible through application of the proper techniques.

HOW TO ATTAIN EQUALIZATION

Equalization can be achieved through a variety of effective means. The circumstances of the negotiation will determine the appropriate point when each might be used successfully. I will discuss five common techniques before concluding with solutions to some special problems.

Advance Positions of Equal or Greater Weight

This technique responds to the requirement, mentioned earlier, that a counter position be of substance. In the yacht illustration, the seller's assertions that the yacht had been completely remodeled and had been once owned by a celebrity were of greater weight than the buyer's original position that the age of the yacht warranted a lower price. And so the balance scale tipped in the seller's favor. Similarly, the buyer in the real estate example countered with a cash offer for the property when the seller brought up her rejection of a previous offer at the same price. The positions were of equal weight, and equalization was achieved.

Demonstrate the Weakness of Your Opponent's Position

Assume the real estate buyer advanced the position that the property was not worth the asking price because its assessed value for tax purposes was only $250,000. Traditionally, these figures are set much lower than the fair market value of the property. By pointing that out in response, the seller would be telling the buyer, in essence, that the buyer's position was not well founded. She would have, thus, completely equalized his position. This is an excellent technique because it is economical, risks nothing, and enhances your prestige at the expense of the other party.

Remove Your Opponent's Position From the Scale

In the real estate example, suppose the seller attempts to justify her $600,000 asking price by declaring that another office parcel recently sold for $1 million. Suppose that million-dollar parcel was twice the size of the property under negotiation. The buyer could easily point this out, distinguish their parcel from the expensive one, and attain equalization. If he fails to do that, however, the seller would feel her position is valid. It would then be very difficult for the buyer to acquire the property for $500,000. Always stuck in the seller's mind would be that other parcel fetching $1 million. No matter that the one going for twice the price is twice as big. It is what the seller believes that is important. The burden is on the buyer to dispel that belief, to put aside her position that the $1-million property is relevant to the one they are negotiating.

Keep Your Opponent Fully Informed

Negotiators are frequently either uninformed or misinformed about facts relative to their task at hand. For instance, the real estate seller may truly believe that the $1-million property is similar to or even the same as the one she has for sale. Maybe she was lazy and didn't investigate the matter. Maybe a friend tipped her off to the $1-million sale without disclosing all the information, or even gave her inaccurate information. Many reasons for the misunderstanding are possible. In this case, it's up to the buyer to enlighten her. The situation highlights the importance, in all cases, of thorough research in any negotiation of importance.

Show the Irrelevance of Your Opponent's Position

In the yacht illustration, the buyer might advance the position that because she intends to use the craft in local waters with a higher than average chemical concentration, the yacht will sustain greater than average deterioration, which will substantially increase her maintenance expenses. Her conclusion: the price should be adjusted downward to take into account that reality. Now, upkeep expenses are a normal and expected part of ownership. Hence, the buyer's argument, while a worthy attempt to lower the price of the boat, is not relevant and does not deserve a place on the equalization balance scale. Here again, however, it is the responsibility of the seller to make that point clear to the buyer. It would be folly for him to assume she knows that. Maybe she does realize the irrelevance of her position, and advancing it is merely a ploy. Maybe it is an innocent mistake. The seller simply cannot take that risk. To attain or maintain equalization, he must establish that position's irrelevance out front in the negotiation.

EQUALIZE EVEN "FAR-OUT" POSITIONS

A special problem in equalization emerges when your opponent advances a position that borders on the ridiculous. I can't emphasize enough the necessity of equalizing even unusual, funny, or absurd negotiating positions. People come in all types and have all manner of beliefs. Once an alien negotiating position is on the table, you cannot permit it to lie there without a response. You cannot assume that an unusual, funny, or absurd position has not been advanced with sincerity by your opponent. Should you fail to equalize that position, it will remain unchallenged in your opponent's mind and thwart your hopes of reaching your objectives.

I recently encountered what could be termed an "irrational" position while negotiating the purchase of a large tract of vacant land. My opponent argued for a greater price for this property because a nearby parcel had sold for a substantially higher price than what I was offering. The problem was that the parcel that sold for substantially more had on it a beautiful new building that made up the bulk of the sale price. I could not assume that my opponent knew that key fact. And even if he did, I couldn't assume that he fully realized that improved land normally sells for more than vacant land, with the increase attributed to the improvements. (As it turned out, he knew about the building but didn't understand its price implications.) The burden was on me to enlighten my opponent and, thereby, equalize his negotiating position.

The necessity of equalizing an opponent's position is a vivid illustration that negotiation is, in the final analysis, mind versus mind. Neutralizing your opponent's mind or altering it toward your way of thinking is your ultimate negotiating quest.

WHY AN OPPONENT MAY HAVE FAILED TO EQUALIZE YOUR POSITIONS

Whenever you advance positions of substance that your opponent fails to equalize, you can safely make certain assumptions. In order to discover which of these possibilities applies, however, you must carefully analyze (1) the facts and circumstances surrounding the negotiation, (2) the subject matter of the negotiation, and, most importantly, (3) the character and ability of your opponent. The three most likely reasons for your opponent's failure are analyzed in the following discussion.

Your Opponent May Have Yielded to Pressure

Pressure is a common reason for a negotiator's failure to equalize. Often in these instances, you can expect your opponent to recover at some point in the proceedings and try to remedy the situation with a belated attempt at equalization. If the negotiation entails numerous sessions, your opponent is more likely to make the attempt. This may very well work to your advantage because you will be facing an opponent on the defensive whose timing has been impaired or lost. Failing to respond to a position in a timely manner almost always works to the guilty party's detriment.

Your Opponent May Be Inexperienced

Another assumption to investigate is that your opponent may lack the experience to appreciate the need to equalize. In these instances, you can repeatedly come back with your unequalized positions over the course of the negotiations until your opponent eventually gives up.

Your Opponent May Lack Relevant Positions of Substance

Another possibility is that your opponent may simply not have the negotiating strength to respond sufficiently to your positions and, thus, be unable to equalize them. This is an ideal situation for you. You will be free to hammer away until your opponent eventually succumbs.

To illustrate, I was negotiating the settlement of a series of lawsuits against a city for what my clients alleged were improper tax assessments made on a large number of principally commercial, office, and multifamily properties. At issue were the values of these properties. Construction was relatively new on most of them and, as a consequence, the income picture was not bright. I, therefore, advanced valuations based upon an income analysis of each property.

The city's representatives at the negotiation failed to respond to my income positions. Instead, they contended that valuation should be based on both the cost of construction and the cost of replacing the properties (often called, naturally enough, "replacement cost"). I quickly equalized their cost and replacement-cost positions by establishing that income was not only the most accurate method of determining fair market value, but also the most widely used and accepted when valuing income-producing properties. Unable to respond adequately, the city negotiators were confined to a defensive stance throughout virtually the entire negotiation. I pounded away at them until I was able to get precisely the valuations I sought.

The Moral Is—

Once your opponent fails to equalize your relevant positions of substance, you have gained a substantial negotiating edge. Therefore, you should be able to easily make accurate assumptions concerning the strength of the opposition; these assumptions will then enable you to formulate and execute the proper negotiating strategies and techniques for the entire negotiation and, thus, attain your negotiating objectives.

CHAPTER 6

Leave Nothing to Chance

Maintaining Control During the Negotiation

Chance favors the prepared mind.

Louis Pasteur

Chance shall not control.

Matthew Arnold

Power flows to the person who knows how.

Elbert Hubbard

Because it lacks rules governing conduct, negotiating can be as uncertain and unpredictable as an oarless canoe trip down a turbulent, white-water river or a saddleless ride on the rodeo's top bucking bronco. Controlling the negotiation, therefore, becomes paramount because lack of control means lack of power. Lack of power, in turn, means lack of negotiating success.

THE UNPREDICTABILITY OF NEGOTIATIONS

To appreciate the sometimes chaotic character of negotiations, consider the following three cases.

The "Silent Chatterboxes"

I once represented a client who was suing her local transit authority. At one of the settlement sessions, my two opponents sat silently like mannequins, animated by only an occasional nod, waiting without expression while I did all the talking. Then, as if a dam within them had suddenly burst, they commenced to speak, flooding the room with torrents of words and making it impossible for me to squeeze in a complete phrase.

Occasionally, I think about that session and ponder what had motivated their strange behavior. Were they "going to school" on me, that is, hoping to pick my brain to learn what I had to offer and to use that information to their advantage? Were they simply inexperienced, proceeding carefully before thrusting themselves wholly into the negotiation? Or was "initial silence followed by a gush of words" their normal mode of negotiating, perhaps some mysterious strategy or technique they felt would give them the edge? No explanation has seemed satisfactory to me. To this day, after all the years I've negotiated professionally, I've never encountered anything like the pair from the transit authority.

The "Angry Paper-Slinger"

In this second case, my opponent seemed to harbor a grudge against the world. His language was rougher than you would expect to hear in an old western saloon, a loser's locker room, or a marine barracks. He was cursing the world, not me. And he was intent on littering the world as well. He'd frequently toss papers around after using them, dropping some on the floor at his feet. As the negotiation progressed, his side of the table began to look as though a hurricane had swept through. In this case, too, I've often wondered whether this fellow's private storm was natural or contrived. Was his showy bad temper just his normal behavior, or was it a deliberate attempt to break my concentration and seize control of the negotiation?

The "Mysteriously Miffed"

In the third case, I faced a negotiator who was angry at me rather than the world. He began the session by declaring that I had insulted him. I was immediately perplexed because that was the very first contact of any sort we'd had; moreover, I carefully avoid insulting anyone because it is no way to "win friends and influence people" (and influencing is the essence of the negotiator's task). I later learned that my "insult" had been delivered in a roundabout way.

I was negotiating a potential purchase by my client of a large, income-producing parcel of commercial real estate that my opponent owned. Previous to the session, I had sent a written offer to the broker who was representing the property owner. In my letter, I explained that my client would be making certain improvements to the property in order to make it more attractive and potentially more lucrative. I contended that the costs of these improvements should be deducted from the asking price. Instead of diplomatically transferring my message by phone, the broker forwarded my letter to the owner. Because he had developed the property according to his personal tastes rather than for the market (which was why the property's profitability was marginal), the owner felt insulted that anyone could even consider making changes in his "baby."

I have, of course, on many, many occasions, run into people with emotional ties to the objects of the negotiation, but never have I encountered an attachment that absorbing. Even the broker, who was present at the meeting, was embarrassed by his client's attitude.

ALWAYS SEEK TO CONTROL THE NEGOTIATIONS

Because of the uncertainty and unpredictability of negotiations, you should always seek to control the negotiation to the greatest degree possible, all the while knowing that complete control is likely beyond your grasp. To reach this goal, you must strive to control every aspect of the negotiation, remembering Napoleon's previously quoted axiom that "In affairs of magnitude . . . everything invariably turns upon a trifle."* In fact, many negotiations do, in fact, turn on trifles.

William James, the philosopher and psychologist, wrote:

> The great thing . . . is to make our nervous system our ally instead of our enemy. . . . For this we must make automatic and habitual . . . as many useful

---

*Emil Ludwig, *Napoleon* (New York: Garden City Publishing Col, 1926), 57.

actions as we can. . . . The more of the details of our daily lives we can hand over to effortless custody automatism, the more our higher powers of mind will be set free for their own proper work.[*]

The application of James's wisdom to negotiations is to seek an environment that offers the greatest mental freedom, where the mind can do its "proper work," namely, where it (you) can seize control. That negotiating environment is comprised of many elements, the discussion of which follows.

Controlling the Location

Where would you have the greatest control—at your opponent's place, at a neutral negotiating site, or your own home field?

Your opponent's home field would be a new, perhaps strange, environment that would require you to adjust mentally at the same time you were attempting to concentrate on the business of negotiation. This division of attention, no matter how slight, would place you at a disadvantage.

Even at a neutral site you will have to make mental adjustments, but so will your opponent. A neutral site is, therefore, some improvement over the enemy's turf. However, your object is not parity, it is control. You want any edge you can get. You want, as the sports writers put it, the home-field advantage.

What I have termed "your home field" is not necessarily restricted to your own office. Any commonly fre-

---

[*]William James, *The Principles of Psychology*, vol. 1 (New York: Dover Publications, 1950), 122.

quented place to which you are fully accustomed, such as a favorite restaurant or even your car, would suffice. You want to be where you are very familiar and comfortable with the surroundings. "Home field" is any place where you enjoy the mental freedom to concentrate on the negotiations.

Negotiating on your home field offers other important advantages that can increase control. At your place, you can break for coffee when you like, or you can have a secretary interrupt at previously designated times. Housekeeping is even a weapon at your disposal. If the other party to the negotiation is a perfectionist, for example, an untidy office with crooked hanging pictures, cigarette-filled ashtrays, and a paper-littered desk might intrude on his or her concentration; that individual might be consciously or subconsciously straightening the papers and pictures during actual discussions. When that occurs, your deliberately unkempt environment is obviously having a disruptive effect that will weaken your guest's concentration and, thus, control and enhance your own.

Controlling the Meeting Schedule

Just as controlling the place of negotiation is important, so is controlling the time to negotiate. We all have a particular schedule on which we function best. Some of us are sharp and alert at the crack of dawn, but our mental batteries run down as the day wears on, so that by later in the afternoon, we are definitely not operating at full mental capacity. For us, negotiating late in the day is a mistake to be avoided if at all possible. In contrast, others of us do not reach our mental peak until late afternoon, and so would hope to ignore the negotiating table until the morning had safely passed. Since mental proficiency is everything in negotiating, controlling the scheduling of sessions is critical.

Controlling the Order of Discussion

When a negotiation involves more than one issue, the order in which the issues are discussed can be important. Thus, influencing the order can afford you significant control over the entire negotiation. You can decide which issues to lead with, which to follow, and when to blend strong issues with weak for balance. A skillful juggling of the order of issues can strengthen the weaker ones and make your overall presentation much more formidable. You might lead with a strong issue to gain the initial momentum, for example. Going next to a weaker issue, followed by another strong one, sandwiches the weakness between strengths and tends to smooth the path towards resolving it in your favor.

A negotiator in control of the order of discussion is like a top baseball pitcher in command of his pitches. The pitcher knows what he is going to throw—fast ball, curve, change-up, and so forth—on any given pitch, as well as where he wants to throw it—inside or outside, high or low. This initiative gives him a decided advantage over the batter, who must guess at what's coming and react as best he can. (That's, in large part, why even the greatest hitters are unsuccessful more than two-thirds of the time.) The pitcher can also exercise some control over the *sequence* of pitches; that is, he can mix in what might be a weak pitch for him amongst his strong ones (fast balls with change-ups, for instance), which makes both seem better and his whole performance even more effective.

Leaving the baseball analogy and returning to the more prosaic world of negotiations, I want to point out that control can even include specifying the dates on which the parties are to meet, when documents are to be sent, and other related matters. Suppose your opponent agrees to supply you with certain documents. It is normally wise for you to tactfully pin down a deadline for receiving them. You can often do this indirectly by setting a time to continue the negotiations, thus necessitating that the documents be sent in ample time for you to review them before the meeting. You will then be able to preplan, and you will have attained a greater degree of control.

OTHER "TRIFLES" IN ESTABLISHING CONTROL

Time, place, and agenda are obvious major elements in controlling a negotiation. However, you can also help yourself by paying attention to a few of the "smaller things."

Scrutinize Documents

Be sure to examine carefully every document that will be given to your opponent. I learned that lesson the hard way when I was negotiating two partnership interests. My opponent refused to concede my position even though he was unable to advance anything to support his stand. No matter how hard I tried, I was unable to make any headway. I kept the pressure on, however, and finally my opponent confessed that he'd been allowed to cull freely through my client's files prior to the time I was retained as negotiator. He had discovered a routine business letter indicating in general terms that the two partnership interests possessed value over and above the net income generated by the partnership assets. Although my opponent was unable to locate any collaborating evidence, the statement in that letter by itself made him very reluctant to reach an agreement. I had to work doubly hard to eventually attain a favorable conclusion.

Avoid Adding New Elements

A new element is virtually any topic that is foreign to the subject matter of the negotiation. Introducing new items broadens the discussions needlessly and also creates an air of uncertainty. This makes control difficult and tends to stifle positive negotiation momentum. A new element can also be a new member added to either of the negotiating teams.

Suppose, for example, you bring a new party—perhaps an associate or client to assist or even audit the proceedings—to a negotiation that is already underway. Not only will the established relationships between the negotiating parties have to be reoriented, your opponent will have an excellent excuse to reopen issues already resolved to your satisfaction. The process is simple. Your new member makes a reference to a settled issue, and your opponent says, "I'm glad you brought that up. I have a problem with . . ." And something you thought you had tucked safely away is back on the table again.

Remember, negotiation is a wide-open affair in which anything can and does happen. I have encountered many, many attempts to reopen issues, even when all written documentation had been signed by all parties.

Watch Your Language

Albert Einstein once remarked that there were some words that "produce such violent disturbance in feelings that the role they play in the transmission of ideas is lost in the background." Words like *criminal, fraud, idiot, jerk, bum,* and similar harsh epithets, carry connotations inappropriate to most negotiations and can, thus, constitute new elements that lead to loss of control. There is no justification for using them.

Emotive language is needlessly and frequently used by some lawyers in pleadings, largely in a misguided attempt to intimidate the other party to the litigation. The tactic usually fails; the only product being anger, which hinders successful settlement. Most often, lawyers guilty of employing unwise language in pleading usually have accepted cases on a contingent fee basis, which means they only get paid if their clients win some money. They hope to extract a settlement, not go to trial. Experienced opposition is likely to recognize the ploy, however, and easily thwart it with a rational response: they calculate the cost of going to trial versus the amount of any settlement, and when settlement negotiations reach a figure *significantly below* the projected trial cost (attorney's fees, time lost, other expenses, and so forth), they agree to the settlement. The harsh language gains nothing but ill will.

FUNNELING

Imagine an ordinary household funnel: a wide circle at the mouth tapering down to a tiny outlet at the bottom. It is ideal for collecting a large volume of something and directing it into a precisely defined (sometimes difficult to reach) location. Funneling is, thus, a controlling activity. It is, in fact, *the most important aspect of attaining negotiating control.* You should strive for funneling from commencement of the negotiation until a final agreement is reached. By applying the technique, you will gradually tighten your control, and when it comes time to close the negotiation (propose and reach an agreement), you will be able to do so smoothly and effectively.

The outset of any negotiation is the widest part of the funnel, because it is here that the greatest latitude is afforded both parties on discussion of the issues. At the beginning of the first session, virtually anything can happen, and your control over the subject matter of the negotiations is minimal. As the discussions progress and agreements are reached on smaller, collateral issues and facts or laws are substantiated, the funnel narrows. The tiny outlet at the bottom of the funnel is the final agreement.

Your goal as a negotiator is to keep the funnel narrowing in such a way that it ends at precisely the point, or negotiated outcome, you want. Unlike using the household funnel, the process is not a simple pour in and hold steady. You will have obstacles to overcome. These are described in the following sections.

Funnel Rewidening

It is not uncommon for new elements to intrude into the negotiation and rewiden the funnel, threatening your control. Sometimes these intrusions are completely unexpected and unavoidable, as in one case I negotiated involving the purchase of commercial/office property. The negotiation had nearly funneled to a conclusion, with only a few minor issues remaining, when suddenly another potential buyer entered the picture. The new party not only made a substantially higher cash offer, but suggested that the entire parcel would be best utilized as an office property alone, rather than a commercial/office combination. Thus, I was faced with three new elements—price, use, and buyer—beyond my control.

My opponent suspended the discussions until he could fully explore the feasibility of making a deal with the new purchaser, only to have the new party withdraw when he discovered his proposal was economically unsound. When the talks resumed, my opponent really wanted to begin all over again. The unexpected intrusion of the potential new purchaser had effectively rewidened the funnel to its fullest, and I was forced to restart the narrowing process. Extra time and effort had to be spent to regain control.

As you gain negotiating experience, you should develop a sense of how to gradually narrow the funnel. Rewidening is an ever-present danger, however, that must be dealt with expeditiously to maintain control of the negotiation and keep it on course to reach the desired conclusion.

Employing Countertactics

I was negotiating a complicated matter in which more than $11 million was in dispute. Because of the large amount of money involved, I knew my opponents would conjure up every conceivable tactic to gain an edge. And they did manage something special.

Negotiations were conducted around a ten-foot-long table. I sat across from Opponent A at one end of the table; Opponent B sat by himself at the other end. He was out of my direct line of sight but still within my lateral or peripheral vision. Opponent A, directly in front of me, conducted the negotiations. Opponent B paid close attention and took every opportunity to peer at my documents on the table next to me, which were within his range of sight. It was an awkward arrangement for me, to say the least, and one I obviously could not allow to continue.

To make matters worse, Opponent A, with whom I was talking, refused to make any agreements, even on the smallest matters, until he had the opportunity to confer with his partner and learn what he had gained from peering at my documents. Opponent A used his colleague's information to supplement his own and widen the discussions.

The burden was on me to counter this tactic as quickly as possible if I expected to successfully funnel the negotiations and attain my objectives. Rather than change my seat and perhaps force my opponents into another bizarre arrangement (which I would have done eventually had nothing else worked), I decided to do something that would take advantage of their split-seating ploy. I requested a short break and used the time to cull my files. I arranged every piece of data that supported my positions in separate piles, freely laying the information on the table in front of me when discussion continued. As I made a point to Opponent A, the supporting data was there for Opponent B to see, substantiating what I was saying. This procedure also allowed me to employ the effective technique of repetition because not only would both opponents hear what I was advocating, but one could see the supporting documents—and he would later relate the contents to his colleague, thus repeating the message again.

Just as importantly, I was controlling the negotiation. By exposing my opponent to only that written information that supported the positions I was advocating orally, I was able to confine discussion largely to that information, allowing us to reach agreement on each issue more easily and quickly, and so narrow the funnel. An added benefit of this hastily improvised strategy was that information gathered in this manner by my opponents was strengthened in their eyes. I, therefore, stayed with this unusual arrangement throughout the numerous sessions of the negotiation.

Postnegotiation Analysis

When you run into a pothole in a road, you make a firm mental note of its location so you don't hit it again. Similarly, at the end of negotiation, it's wise to note and

analyze every unexpected hole and bump in the negotiating experience. Focus on the occasions where matters got out of hand (the funnel either failed to narrow
or even rewidened). The reasons often are the introduc-
tion of new elements or information irrelevant to the
session's issues (the opponent was allowed to escape
from the confines of the narrowing funnel).

Reflect on how you coped with the new elements and
regained control, or how you will do so the next time.
Think about how you got your opponent back under
control, or how you plan to do so when you next meet?
Let your considered experiences teach you how to funnel, the most important aspect of control.

KEEPING RESOLVED ISSUES CLOSED

Reopening issues already resolved is commonplace and
frequently, as related, even extends to fully documented
and signed agreements. When that happens, the funnel
begins to widen again and control is loosened. My experience indicates that people unskilled in the art of negotiation are the most prone to reopening closed issues.
Being unsure of themselves, they have second, third, and
even fourth thoughts about the wisdom of their decisions. So they seek to unsettle that which has already
been settled.

When faced with this problem, a surprisingly effective solution is to simply and tactfully remind your opponent that the issue has been fully resolved. Usually
that is enough to get your opponent's thinking back on
track and, thus, keep the funnel narrowed. However, an
opponent might *insist* on reopening an issue. Deft handling is called for, but not alarm. The best approach is
to review, in detail if necessary, the matters in question
to satisfy your opponent that they indeed have been
resolved. If, at this point, your opponent is really dissat-

isfied instead of merely plagued by self-doubts, you have two viable options. You can either stand on the previously reached agreements, or you can renegotiate. If you are forced to renegotiate, the funnel will undoubtedly rewiden.

There are a number of other reasons why an opponent may want to renegotiate. Circumstances could have changed since the issues were resolved, some information may not have been included, or peers or superiors might be exerting pressure to cut a better deal. Whatever the reason, the best approach is to review the matter in detail. That will usually satisfy your opponent and retain the narrowness of the funnel and your control. In fact, freely reviewing matters at your opponent's request or insistence will bolster your credibility. The greater your credibility, the more likely your opponent will accept your advanced positions, with less substantiation. As a result, you can more readily narrow the funnel, control the negotiations, and reach your objectives—which is, in the final analysis, your ultimate goal.

You should, therefore, work to become adept at funneling in order to gain control of the negotiations and constantly seek negotiating control in order to succeed. Negotiating is an art form but not an end in itself. The end is getting what you want or what the party you represent wants.

CHAPTER 7

Don't Get Painted into a Corner

How to Make Offers and Counteroffers

> *I'll make him an offer he can't refuse.*
>
> Mario Puzo
> (*The Godfather*)

> *When you have spoken the word, it reigns over you. When it is unspoken, you reign over it.*
>
> Arabian proverb

Offers and counteroffers are two distinct facets of negotiation. The *offer begins* the process of *finalizing* a negotiation. *Counteroffers* facilitate that process by *narrowing* the *differences* between the negotiating sides. Both offers and counteroffers are fraught with dangers that can and often do lead to serious negotiating mistakes, frequently with devastating consequences for the erring party. To illustrate, look again at the Rockefeller-Morgan negotiation.

THE OFFER: LESSONS FROM THE RICH AND FAMOUS

Rockefeller-Morgan

You'll remember that when financial titan J. P. Morgan had acquired control of the production and manufacture of steel after buying out Andrew Carnegie, he was still in dire need of ore fields, which were controlled by John D. Rockefeller. Recall, as well, that John D. had informed Morgan that he had retired from business and J. P. would have to deal with John, Jr. When Morgan and the younger Rockefeller finally met, John, Jr., was faced with Morgan's demand to name a price for the ore fields. John, Jr., replied: "I have no information that he [John D.] wishes to dispose of his ore properties; in point of fact, I am confident that he has no such desire."[*]

Morgan's demand that John, Jr., name a price was a shrewd move. He wanted the youthful, relatively inexperienced negotiator (John, Jr., was only 27 at the time) to set, in effect, the upper price limit, the maximum

---

[*]John K. Winkler, *Incredible Carnegie* (New York: The Vanguard Press, 1931), 269.

Rockefeller could receive for the ore fields. Morgan could then counter with a lower figure and hope to arrive at a price somewhere between the two, but certainly lower than, opening price quoted by John, Jr.

The young man did not take the bait, however. By refusing to make the initial offer, he hit the ball right back into Morgan's court. The financier knew he had been stymied, and he remained silent rather than lead with an offer. Thus, the initial meeting ended, but both parties knew that Morgan still needed the ore fields and would have to make the next move.

When John, Jr., reported to his father, the elder Rockefeller meditated for an instant and advised his son, ". . . (I)f I had been in your place, I should have done precisely what you did."*

Meanwhile, Morgan had decided on his next approach: he would call in Henry Clay Frick to assist in the negotiations. Rockefeller respected Frick and agreed to meet with him. At the meeting, he told Frick he wasn't seeking to sell his ore fields but wouldn't stand in Morgan's way if Morgan needed them. This, of course, was an excellent strategy. By establishing Morgan's need and his own indifference, Rockefeller had set the stage for demanding a premium price for the ore fields. The refusal by John, Jr., to set a price and, thereby, put a ceiling on negotiations also contributed to Morgan's difficult position.

But Rockefeller wasn't finished yet. First, he got Frick to admit that the ore fields were quite valuable properties. He then astonished Frick by asking for his assistance in getting a fair price. As a go-between for Morgan, Frick was naturally hesitant about representing Rockefeller.

---

*John K. Winkler, *Incredible Carnegie* (New York: The Vanguard Press, 1931), 269.

But John D. had an answer: "You need not hesitate, Mr. Frick," Rockefeller assured him calmly. "My confidence is implicit. You will receive no complaint from me."[*]

As it turned out, Rockefeller received $5 million more than Morgan had contemplated paying for the ore fields. With John, Jr., adroitly refusing to make an opening offer and John D. skillfully employing Frick the negotiation succeeded admirably.

James J. Ling

When James Ling was president of Ling-Temco-Vought, Inc., he negotiated the sale of a company called Computer Tech, which the corporation owned. The prospective purchaser was a large insurance company. Ling expected an opening offer between $60 and $65 million. He would counter with $85 million, and the parties would settle for a price of $75 to $80 million. Like Rockefeller, Ling wisely refrained from naming a figure at the beginning of the negotiations. The insurance company made the first offer, and, when it came, Ling had a difficult time keeping a straight face. The insurance company's initial offer was $90 million.

The Moral of the Stories

Both the Rockefeller and Ling experiences illustrate the most sound, yet frequently violated principle of making offers: let the other guy go first. The principle has two potential benefits: first, as in the Ling case, the opponent's

---

[*]John K. Winkler, *Incredible Carnegie* (New York: The Vanguard Press, 1931), 269.

initial offer may be substantially greater than anticipated, which is always a pleasant experience; second, by
leading with an offer, the other side has either set an
upper limit to what it expects to sell for or a lower limit
to what it expects to buy for. The insurance company's
opening offer established $90 million as the lower limit
to what it could expect to pay for Ling's company, Computer Tech. Ling could use that offer as a base from
which to negotiate upwards, which would have constituted a considerable advantage for him as the seller.

If, on the other hand, Ling had violated the principle
and led with a figure of $85 million, he would have set
the upper limit for what he could have expected to receive
for Computer Tech, because he would have provided an
opportunity for the insurance company to negotiate down
to a figure lower than $85 million, a considerable advan-
tage for it as the buyer. In fact, since the insurance
company knew Computer Tech was up for sale, it should
have insisted that Ling make the initial offer. As is so
often the case in negotiation, however, that golden opportunity was lost.

In the Rockefeller-Morgan negotiations, both sides
recognized the advantage of the other making the initial
offer. The burden was on Morgan, however, because both
sides knew he was in need of the ore fields. Thus, when
his ploy to induce the younger Rockefeller to make the
first move failed, Morgan's hand was forced, and the
Rockefellers gained the edge.

Both cases demonstrate the wisdom of letting the
other side make the initial offer. The insurance company's
failure to heed that basic principle cost it millions. Even
had the company bid lower than Ling expected, he would
not have suffered greatly. He could have simply made a
higher counteroffer; the initiative, and the advantage,
was still his. From the opposite point of view, if a seller
makes an opening offer that is higher than the buyer
expected, the buyer can still claim the edge by

counteroffering with a lower figure. An unexpectedly high or low figure only compounds the initial error of making the opening offer.

For example, the insurance company could have opened with $40 million, well below Ling's expectations for an initial bid of $60-$65 million and his target price of $75-$80 million. Had Ling determined that the $40-million bid was the insurance company's way of fishing for a bargain, he could have countered with a $90-$100 million price. That would have signaled the company to respond with a counteroffer of its own much higher than $40 million if it was serious about acquiring Computer Tech.

Having your opponent lead with an offer places you in a "win-win" situation. If that initial offer is higher than you expect, as in the Ling case, you are ahead at the outset. If it is lower, you have the opportunity to counteroffer with a figure that will bring your opponent's thinking up to your price range. Either way, the advantage is yours.

ALWAYS EXPLAIN THE BASIS FOR ANY OFFER

You will be in negotiations where it is not possible to get your opponent to make the initial offer. Morgan certainly was in that position with Rockefeller. The insurance company in the Ling case, on the other hand, could have easily pressured Ling to make his opening offer because Computer Tech was up for sale. The seller is frequently in that situation. Most often, in fact, a selling price is immediately attached to an asset when it is placed on the market. Real estate, for example, normally is listed at a definite price. In effect, the initial offer has already been made.

But even when the selling price is posted, you should not begin negotiations without providing a strong explanation of the basis for that asking price. Such an unsubstantiated figure is called a "bare" or "naked" price. If you lead with a bare or naked price, you invite your opponent to respond with a substantially lower counteroffer. Bare selling prices can become very costly as the negotiations progress, unless there is a great demand for the asset up for sale.

Consequently, you must endeavor to "clothe" your offer by justifying it when you first sit down for face-to-face negotiations. You must explain to your opponent the basis or reasons, for the listed price. If you give adequate support for your opening price, you will make it more difficult for your opponent to justify a significantly lower counteroffer. Thus, you will be closer to meeting your negotiating objectives, that is, to obtaining the price you want for what you have for sale.

MY WHISKEY JUG QUEST

Being an antique buff, I searched a long time for an old, authentic, ceramic, gallon whiskey jug of the kind immortalized in the classic *Ma and Pa Kettle* hillbilly movies. I unexpectedly ran across precisely the jug I was after at a flea market at a midwestern resort. The sticker price was $18. The seller made no attempt to justify the offering price, thus providing me with complete freedom to negotiate downwards. The dialogue went as follows:

ILICH: I like the jug. Nice dust collector for the corner of a room. (This establishes that I have no key need for the item, which might have made the seller hold firm on the offering price.) Price is a little high for my purposes, though.

SELLER: How much do you have in mind?

ILICH: Three to four dollars.

SELLER: *(After reflection)*. I'd like to move it, but that's pretty low. (Seller should not have disclosed desire to sell, providing me with negotiating power.)

ILICH: How about five?

SELLER: Make it ten. That's $8 off.

ILICH: I don't want to pay too much. It's going to sit someplace in my house. How about seven?

SELLER: Okay. (Accepting $7 rather than $7.50, which would split the difference between my $5 and the seller's $10, substantiated the seller's desire to make the sale.)

If the seller had provided reasons of substance to justify the offering price, I would have found it difficult to warrant my substantially lower counteroffer. My only hope to justify a lower price would have been to find arguments to either equalize the seller's position or surpass it in weight.

The same principles apply whether the negotiation concerns inexpensive items at a flea market or assets worth millions of dollars. When you are forced to make an initial offer, you must provide a detailed explanation of the basis for that offer. Failure to do so invites a substantially lower counteroffer. On the other hand, if you have laid a solid basis, your opponent will find it extremely difficult to respond with a substantially lower counteroffer without introducing some material basis for that substantially lower counteroffer.

To illustrate, consider what would have transpired had the seller of the jug established a basis for the $18 offering price. He might have asserted that the jug was in mint condition (which it was), sold for $30 to $50 in area stores (which it did), and was authentic (which it was), not merely a manufactured prop. I would have had a much harder time making such a low countering price.

Indeed, faced with that solid explanation of the jug's value, I would have had to raise my initial counteroffer, probably substantially, in order to ultimately make the purchase.

THE COUNTEROFFER

Counteroffers are a highly important and effective facet of negotiation. Yet, counteroffers frequently are not only misunderstood but unused. In fact, it is not uncommon to have one side, displeased with all or a portion of an offer on the negotiating table, simply walk away when, with finesse and skillful use of counteroffers, they could have obtained excellent results. Moreover, many negotiators who do use counteroffers fail to understand both their legal significance and practical effects.

Another Real Estate Example

Early in my negotiating career, I learned an important lesson concerning the value of and problems with counteroffers. A client had made several offers to purchase a large parcel of real estate he wanted to develop. The property was not listed for sale, and the property owner never responded to my client's offers, despite his several attempts to get a reaction. I was asked to visit the property owner to see whether the sale could be completed.

The property owner was very happy with the price and all the other material aspects of my client's offer, but he had a problem with my client taking possession ten days after the closing. The owner lived on the property and wanted ample time to find another suitable residence; it was as simple as that. Since the owner desired to avoid the expense of retaining either a broker or an attorney to represent him in the transaction, I suggested he put in writing precisely what he wanted out of the sale, and I would present it to my client. In other words, I invited him to make a counteroffer.

Because he was relatively inexperienced in business matters, it had never occurred to the owner to counter my client's offer with his own terms for selling the property. Moreover, since his main concern (occupancy until he could find another place to live) was personal and very important to him, he believed my client's proposal to take possession ten days after closing must have been a business necessity. In fact, the ten-day possession position is common in many real estate transactions; no business necessity existed.

The property owner did make a counteroffer accepting my client's terms but proposing a 90-day occupancy period after closing. My client countered with the provision that should the owner find a suitable residence in less than 90 days, then my client could take possession on the day the former owner moved. The property owner accepted, and both parties were happy. The counteroffers had facilitated the finalization of the sale.

LEGAL RAMIFICATIONS OF COUNTEROFFERS

Although there are variations from state to state, the law regarding counteroffers is basically the same across the country. If a counteroffer deviates from the previous offer in even the smallest way, it constitutes a rejection of the *entire* offer, and the counteroffer becomes, in essence, a new offer.

For example, a buyer offers to purchase a home for $300,000, provided the sale is closed within 60 days and the seller pays for all closing costs, a termite inspection, and the cost of testing the well water for purity. The seller likes everything about the offer, except he wants 65 days before closing. He, therefore, says to the buyer: "I accept, but I need five more days for closing." Do they have a binding agreement? No.

Why not? The imposition of the additional five-day period constitutes a rejection of the buyer's entire offer. If she refuses to accept that additional five-day period, the seller cannot then drop that requirement and accept her offer by agreeing to her 60-day closing. Once modified by a counteroffer, the original offer is gone, unless, of course, the *buyer chooses to renew it*.

The Buyer's and Seller's Options

In addition to renewing her original offer, the buyer has other options available. The buyer can: (1) simply reject the seller's counteroffer and walk away from the deal; (2) accept the seller's counteroffer, in which case they have a deal; or (3) make a counteroffer to the seller's counteroffer, in which case the seller's counteroffer is rejected.

Assume the buyer agrees to accept the 65-day period but cuts the offering price to $295,000. That change constitutes a rejection of the *seller's* entire counteroffer, even though the portion of the deal being rejected (the $300,000) originated with the buyer. The seller now has the same options the buyer had when she considered his counteroffer to her original offer. The seller can: (1) reject and walk, (2) accept as is and make the deal, or (3) make another counteroffer, which automatically rejects the buyer's counteroffer.

This process can, and often does, continue for an extended period.

A Foray into the World of Television

A television production company threatened to sue an advertising agency to recover the costs of making some commercials. The producer's position was that it had a binding contract with the agency to produce the commercials, and so the necessary expenditures were authorized. My client, the agency, denied a contract existed.

As is frequently the case in a hectic industry, neither one of the warring parties could locate a formal document authorizing the production of the commercials. The only written evidence was a two-inch-thick file of chaotic correspondence that had been exchanged over a six-month period between the producer and the agency.

Good sense, of course, would have dictated that a formal contract be executed before work even began on the commercials, especially when expenditures were anticipated to (and did) exceed $100,000. In the real business world, however, deadlines and payrolls must be met in the heat of fierce competition, and the clarity of hindsight is not always available at decision-making time.

To succeed in any potential legal action, the production company would have to show breach of either an actual or implied contract with the agency. The key question thus became: Did the parties, in the process of accumulating that mass of correspondence, manage to enter into a binding contract? The answer depended entirely upon whether there was a legitimate acceptance of a counteroffer.

In an attempt to answer that vital question, I put the correspondence into chronological order from the first day of negotiations to the last and carefully read each letter. Each successive letter modified the other side's proposal, sometimes minutely. Each alteration, however, constituted a new counteroffer and, thus, a rejection of the other side's preceding counteroffer. At times, the parties were extremely close to finalizing an agreement, but always a slight change kept the arrangement from becoming a set contract.

In the producer's final letter to the agency, a single sentence proposed a slight alteration to our client's latest counteroffer. That slight alteration constituted a new counteroffer and a rejection of the agency's counteroffer. Further, because the agency did not respond within a reasonable time after receiving the producer's last counteroffer, that also was rejected. There was no contract. Nor did the producer by proceeding to make the commercials, revive or create an actual or implied contract.

We apprised the production company of our findings, noting especially the critical sentence in the final letter. The producer dropped all demands for payment rather than incur the costs of what would likely be unsuccessful litigation.

The producer's unfortunate experience illustrates vividly the need to understand fully the nature of counteroffers. Again, *a counteroffer is a complete and final rejection of an offer or counteroffer*. You cannot make a counteroffer, have it rejected, and then change your mind and accept the offer or counteroffer you just turned down. You have lost that option, unless the other party revives the rejected offer. That's why you must consider very carefully every aspect of every offer or counteroffer and, if necessary, seek additional information or clarification from the other party before deciding how to respond.

THE VARIED USES OF COUNTEROFFERS

Counteroffers have a number of excellent applications in negotiation. As previously noted, the counteroffer facilitates the finalizing process initiated by the original offer. Therefore, should you wish to reject your opponent's offer or counteroffer, you should do so by making your own counteroffer and, thus, keep the negotiation rolling. Your counteroffer tactfully says that you have fully considered your opponent's offer (or counteroffer) and found it not quite acceptable—but here is how you would like to make the deal. Responding to your counteroffer is much easier for your opponent than coping with outright rejection, which would require walking away from the deal or swallowing hard and coming up with a new offer, neither of which is conducive to the negotiation process.

Surprisingly, price is not often the stumbling block in a negotiation. Other terms and conditions will frequently hinder an agreement. A typical real estate transaction, for example, entails many other negotiable matters besides price. Answers must be found to such questions as: How is the purchase price to be paid: cash in full? a partial downpayment with the balance payable over a number of years? If the latter, how much is the downpayment: 20 percent? 50 percent? In how many years is the balance to be paid off: 3? 5? 20? How much interest is payable on the unpaid balance: 8 percent? 10 percent? Who pays for a survey of the property? Counteroffers can play a vital role in resolving these issues once the parties have agreed on the purchase price.

COUNTEROFFERS ARE A FORM OF CONTROL

Negotiation is essentially a ruleless, and sometimes a ruthless, activity. Therefore, you must, as previously related, do what is necessary to exercise control over the negotiations. Control is power. Counteroffers are a form of control because they provide you with the opportunity to put forth acceptable terms and conditions. You force your opponent to think about what *you* want on the issues.

To illustrate, suppose someone offers $60,000 for a lot that you own, with a 20 percent down payment and the $48,000 balance payable over 5 years at 8 percent interest. The price is lower than you want and the 5-year payoff is too long. Rather than reject the offer outright, however, you wisely choose to counteroffer with the terms you desire. Assume you come back with a $70,000 purchase price payable over 3 years, with 30 percent down and 10 percent interest on the $49,000 balance. You and the prospective buyer are now in a range for both price and payment terms to continue the negotiation. The burden has shifted to the buyer, however, to either accept your counteroffer or to make a counteroffer closer to your terms in order to close the deal.

To facilitate the control gained through your counteroffer, you must explain the basis for the counteroffer in sufficient detail to justify it to your opponent and to make it more difficult for your opponent to reject it. In that way, you not only make your rejection of your opponent's original offer more palatable to him or her, you also establish your sincerity. You are now building a bridge of trust, the ideal relationship for a negotiation. When the parties trust each other, the road toward a successful, negotiated outcome is smoothed.

AVOID POLARIZATION

Offers and counteroffers should be structured and conveyed so as to provide the flexibility that negotiation demands. It is normally unwise to make an ultimatum part of an offer or counteroffer. Ultimatums foster resentment and even anger, which works against obtaining your objectives. Further, ultimatums are restrictive. Once you issue an ultimatum, you'll find it difficult, if not impossible, to change your mind. And you'll want to be able to alter your counteroffer if new information or changed circumstances warrant.

Declaring "This is my final offer; take it or leave it" makes it almost impossible for your opponent to propose counteroffers, even if so inclined. Negotiation progress is halted because neither one of you has an option. A negotiator with no options has virtually no power—he is like a boat adrift at sea with a dead motor, no sail, no oars. If you issue an ultimatum and, for whatever reason, change your mind and submit a new counteroffer, your opponent will likely conclude your ultimatum was a bluff. Not only will your opponent fail to take seriously any future ultimatums you might issue, anything of substance you put forth might be similarly discounted. At that point, your chances of attaining your negotiating objectives are slim or nonexistant.

How to Convey an Ultimatum if Necessary

Ultimatums are as dangerous as loaded guns. But sometimes they are necessary, and it is possible to use them with a degree of safety. Should you need to convey an ultimatum with an offer or counteroffer, avoid using words or phrases of finality. The best method I have found is to simply state the terms of the offer and explain precisely why it would not be possible to alter those terms *unless* some new material facts or circumstances arise that warrant an alteration.

This approach hits the ball back into the opponent's court but in such a way that permits you both the chance to keep playing. You have been firm but tactful, alleviating the risk that your opponent will become resentful or angry at receiving an ultimatum. The burden is on your opponent to either (1) accept your offer or counteroffer, (2) reject it, or (3) respond to your *unless* by revealing new facts or circumstances that would materially affect your proposal. You then have the opportunity to scrutinize this new information, with the realization that your opponent's taking the time to find it means the desire to conclude the negotiation is strong. That strong desire provides you with excellent negotiating power. Furthermore, if the new facts or circumstances are legitimate, you have a genuine basis for altering your offer without loss of prestige or power. In other words, you have expressed your ultimatum in a way that allows you to change your mind without penalty.

What I have called the *language of finality* can creep into an offer or counteroffer if you are not careful and can perhaps indirectly and unintentionally polarize negotiations as surely as a baldly stated ultimatum. The following are examples of words and phrases that tend to stifle negotiating process: *absolutely, never, no, can't, won't, refuse to budge,* and *unlikely to.* Avoid them and similar words and phrases of finality. Express your offer or counteroffer with a careful ear for the words you choose. Your terms should be clear to the other party and your language unprovocative. You want agreement, not anger.

Stay Cool

You do not want to become angry if your offer or counteroffer is rejected. Anger is a polarizing emotion. Angry people, as related, never cower in a corner; nor are they timid or afraid. Angry people have the confidence of the obsessed, driven by the need to strike back at the source of their anger. Even timid people made angry become forceful and say and do things they normally would not. Their reason distorted by emotion, they make mistakes. Anger, unless a deliberate negotiating strategy and fully justified under the particular negotiating circumstances, is the enemy of negotiation. It stops progress as abruptly as a head-on collision.

AVOID LOWBALLING OR HIGHBALLING

Making excessively low or high offers or counteroffers is almost always a mistake. You jeopardize your credibility and run the risk of gaining a reputation for lowballing or highballing that can have long-term harmful effects; that is, other negotiators may stop taking you seriously, which will dissipate your negotiating power and all but eliminate your chances of attaining your negotiating objectives.

Another danger of making an excessively low or high offer or counteroffer is that it can often lead to large initial concessions, which, in turn, usually result in negotiation failure. For example, a buyer makes an offer of $1 million for a business that's clearly worth $5 million in hopes that the seller will counteroffer for substantially less than $5 million. More likely, however, the seller, particularly if an experienced negotiator, will consider the $1 million offer to be both unrealistic and insincere and reject it outright. With no counteroffer on the table, the potential buyer will be faced with the unfortunate and self-inflicted dilemma of either walking away from the negotiation a failure or substantially increasing the original offer. Assume the buyer really wants the business and, thus, increases the bid to $3 million. That's a major concession early in the negotiation, and it is highly doubtful, assuming again that the seller is an experienced negotiator, that the buyer will acquire the desired asset for an amount materially lower than $5 million.

HOW TO TREAT YOUR OPPONENT'S OFFERS AND COUNTEROFFERS

Be absolutely certain you understand the precise terms and conditions of any offers and counteroffers your opponent makes. If you do not understand something, ask for a clarification. This rule is particularly vital when responding to oral offers and counteroffers. Oral offers and counteroffers are common, and can frequently lead to disagreement, misunderstanding, and, ultimately, to negotiation failure. The best policy, of course, is to have your opponent put all offers and counteroffers in writing.

However, that is often impractical for a variety of reasons. The negotiations may be rushed, with no time for written documents at the offer or counteroffer stage. Perhaps you and your opponent have exchanged offers orally on previous occasions dealing with similar matters and so established a precedent. Maybe your opponent will resent being asked to put an oral offer into writing. Finally, you may face a negotiator who prefers to arrive at the written stage only when an agreement has been fully consummated and so will refuse your request. Should any of these conditions or others exist, you will have to rely on the oral transmission of offers and counteroffers. Listen carefully and ask questions.

My Two-Step Approach

When engaged in a negotiation where it is not possible to have all the offers in writing, I normally take two steps during or immediately after an oral offer or counteroffer has been made.

1. I ask for a clarification of any terms or provisions that may be unclear to me or that I believe need further explanation. For example, in a negotiation for the construction of a large commercial building, my discussions with the prospective tenant contained only oral offers and counteroffers, with the final agreement to be put in writing after all the terms and conditions had been settled. In addition to the normal building outlays, the tenant wanted to add soft costs to the total cost of construction. Since the term *soft* in that context can have a variety of meanings, I asked for a precise definition with examples of what constituted soft costs in order to avoid any misunderstandings.

Language, especially English, is very susceptible to numerous interpretations. I often think of President

Carter's problem when he was negotiating a Middle East peace settlement with Egypt's President Anwar Sadat and Israel's Prime Minister Menacham Begin. President Carter revealed later that he was never far from a good dictionary and thesaurus so he could search for acceptable meanings for such terms as *autonomy*, *self-rule*, *devolution*, *authority*, and *minor modifications*.

2. Having clarified terms and provisions, I repeat the specifics of the offer or counteroffer to my opponent, seeking an affirmative response to indicate we are in complete agreement on the *meaning* of the offer or counteroffer now on the table. Thus acknowledged, the specifics of the offer are now firmly imbedded in my opponent's mind, which makes it difficult for him or her to deny or attempt to alter them later. I try to obtain that acknowledgement in a tactful manner so as not to affront my opponent's integrity. I often put the burden on myself by saying, for example, "I want to be sure I fully understand what we're talking about here so that I don't fumble the ball."

People are sensitive to any perceived slight that might reflect adversely on their integrity. An easy-going approach like the one I have suggested will tend to eliminate any danger that your opponent will feel affronted by your desire to pin down the terms of an oral offer or counteroffer.

WHEN THEY LOWBALL OR HIGHBALL YOU

How do you handle excessively high or low offers and counteroffers? Suppose, for example, you have listed a home for sale at $100,000, and someone approaches you with an offer of only $20,000. Obviously, there is a problem. The key to solving the problem is to determine the prospective buyer's motivation for making such a low offer. You can ask, but there is no assurance that you'll get an answer or, if you do, that it will be accurate. You can make assumptions based upon the facts and circumstances surrounding the transaction. Perhaps the buyer has no genuine intention of acquiring the home and is merely taking a shot at possibly getting it for a fraction of its true worth. Chances are, however, the individual lacks knowledge of the real value of the asset, which is often the case in these situations.

When you receive an excessive offer or counteroffer, it is vital that you do not let yourself become angry. (Remember, anger is a polarizing emotion that either stifles or stops negotiations.) Ask your opponent to explain the basis for the offer or counteroffer. If your opponent is ill-informed on the relevant facts and circumstances, take the opportunity to enlighten him or her and to solicit a new, more suitable offer or counteroffer. In those very few cases where your opponent is deliberately being unreasonable, you still should explain why the excessive offer is unacceptable. An opponent with serious intentions will alter the offer. If the individual refuses to do so, you can decide whether there is any legitimate reason for continuing the negotiation. But be certain there is absolutely no reason to continue before you break off the discussions and terminate this chance to reach your negotiating objectives.

THE "GO-TO-SCHOOL" INTEREST

Frequently in the business world, one company will express a desire to purchase another when the real motive is to "go to school" on (learn about) the other company. The company pretending to seek an acquisition is calculating that a lot of valuable information can be picked up during the course of the negotiations. This technique targets, in particular, privately owned businesses on which little or no public information is available. Fortunately for the company being pursued, this artificial interest can be detected easily at the offer-counteroffer stage. That is one reason why, when I represent a "sought" company in this position, I try to arrive at the offer stage as early as possible, even if the prospective "purchaser" has agreed to place in escrow a substantial nonrefundable sum in the event a purchase is not consummated. The offer acts as a barometer by which one can gauge the sincerity and genuineness of the alleged buyer's intent. If they lowball, they're probably insincere, and I can proceed as indicated above to protect my client company.

This case illustrates once again the value of understanding how offers and counteroffers function in negotiations.

CHAPTER 8

You Have 10 Minutes to Decide

Take Full Advantage of the Opportunity to Set Deadlines

What we see depends mainly on what we look for.

John Lubbock

Knowledge and human power are synonymous.

Bacon

Deadlines are a powerful negotiating weapon. When used skillfully, they can achieve astonishing results, as two familiar cases will illustrate.

MORGAN AND GATES

After J. Pierpont Morgan's interests bought out Andrew Carnegie in the process of organizing United States Steel, Morgan proceeded to meet with other industry leaders to work out terms for acquiring their companies. One such firm was represented by John W. Gates. Gates began his career as a barbed-wire salesman. He rented a small parcel of land in Texas, built a barbed-wire corral, and then challenged any rancher to find a steer that could escape from the corral. None could. Gates received so many orders that he abandoned his employer and started his own highly successful wire business, American Steel & Wire. He became known as "bet-a-million" Gates because of his propensity for high-stakes gambling. He was reputed to have once spent a rainy day on a train betting a companion on which raindrops coursing down a windowpane would reach the bottom first. The bet was $1,000 a race.*

Long hours of negotiating between Gates and Judge Elbert H. Gary, Morgan's representative, failed to reach an agreement on the acquisition of American Steel & Wire. Morgan did not participate in the discussions, preferring to wait in his office, which was in the building where Gates and Gary were meeting. Finally, Gary left the session to advise Morgan that the negotiations with Gates were hopelessly deadlocked with no likelihood of reaching an agreement. *Completely out of other options,*

---

*Frederick Lewis Allen, *The Great Pierpont Morgan* (New York: Harper & Brothers, 1949), 164–65.

Morgan decided to try a desperate tact. At Gary's suggestion, Morgan went to the meeting room and confronted Gates. His message was brief and to the point: he was leaving for home in ten minutes, and, if they didn't reach an agreement by then, the matter would be closed. Morgan and his colleagues would build their own plant to compete with American Steel & Wire. Gates capitulated.

I want to stress here, on the heels of the discussion on ultimatums, that Morgan's tactic was justified in this situation; he had *completely* exhausted all other negotiating options. Even then, his ultimatum worked because he was wise enough to tie it to a deadline and employ fear of competition as a powerful ally.

THE IRANIAN HOSTAGES

Deadline setting also proved the key to obtaining release of the 52 Americans held hostage by Iran for over 14 months. Jimmy Carter was about to leave office and Ronald Reagan assume the presidency. Deputy Secretary of State Warren M. Christopher was still trying to reach an agreement with Iran. Throughout the entire time the hostages had been held captive, U. S. negotiators failed to instill a sense of urgency in the Iranians by establishing a deadline. However, Carter was soon to depart, and an unknown factor, Reagan, was about to come on the scene. The Iranians unquestionably understood what that kind of change could mean and became more serious about reaching a settlement. Christopher was able to take advantage of this change in mood.

He advised the Algerian officials who were acting as middlemen in the negotiations that his authority would expire the next day when Reagan was sworn in as president. To dramatize the significance of the impending deadline, Christopher ordered his state department plane readied for departure at noon, Washington time, the next day, when the Carter administration would end. The Algerians swiftly notified Iran of this new development, and the hostage crisis was resolved over the next 18 hours. One top state department aide remarked: "The exercise proved that deadlines work."* They do indeed.

WHY DEADLINES WORK

There are three important reasons why deadlines play such a significant role in negotiation. Each reason, in and of itself, justifies using deadlines. Be advised, however, that setting a deadline is like swinging a two-edged sword—it cuts both ways. If not properly used, deadlines can do your position more harm than good.

Deadlines Create Anxiety in Your Opponent

The Morgan-Gates and Iranian-hostage experiences illustrate this most important benefit of proper deadline use. Anyone nervy enough to make chancy and pricey bets with steers and raindrops is obviously not prone to panic. But faced with a ten-minute deadline and the prospect of brutal competition from Morgan, Gates became very anxious indeed. Upon receiving Morgan's deadline, Gates turned to a colleague and remarked: "I don't know whether the old man means that or not." When assured by Gary that Morgan was dead serious, Gates replied, "Then I guess we will have to give up."†

Also not prone to panic, the Iranians became anxious

---

*Time, February 2, 1981, 37.
†Frederick Lewis Allen, The Great Pierpont Morgan (New York: Harper & Brothers, 1949), 177.

when confronted suddenly with the unknown. Christopher's very plausible deadline occasioned by the changing of leaders gave a sense of urgency to the proceedings and convinced the Iranians that their best interests lay in reaching an agreement rather than face the uncertainty of dealing with a new administration.

Statistics reveal that most agreements are reached at or near a deadline. For example, a substantial number of lawsuits are settled "on the courthouse steps" before the "deadline" of going to trial is reached. As trial time looms, the anxiety levels of the lawyers for both the plaintiff and the defendant increase; they fear not only losing the case but simply standing before a judge and jury. Since courtroom anxiety is inversely proportional to courtroom experience, attorneys with little time logged in front of a judge and jury tend to be overwhelmed with fear to the point of making substantial concessions in settlement.

I can vividly recall an attorney who rarely did courtroom work but who was compelled by circumstances to try a case. Fear of the impending trial (the deadline) caused him to drink heavily, and even before he reached the courthouse steps, his breath was rich with the aroma of liquor. As trial time approached, he capitulated and settled the case. Such happenings are not as rare as you might think. Contrary to popular myth, lawyers are quite human and, thus, motivated by their personal fears.

One of our interesting human attributes is fear of the unknown. That fear usually prompts us to take evasive action. In the grip of fear, all the possibilities, especially the negative and harmful ones, dance in our minds. And as the time when we must face the source of our fear (the deadline) draws nearer, we imagine the worst. We worry; we fret; we agonize. In order to get relief, we begin to consider how to eliminate the cause of our problem. If the cause is a negotiation deadline, we usually seek compromise as the quickest solution.

Compromise settlement was Gates' way out when he had only ten minutes to reach an agreement or face the unknown of Morgan's threat. Gates undoubtedly feared the worst, that competition from Morgan might even drive American Steel & Wire out of business. The Iranians' fear of the unknown centered on the question of what the new Reagan administration would do. Carter they understood. Aside from an unsuccessful helicopter rescue mission, Carter had firmly established himself as an essentially predictably nonviolent opponent. Reagan, on he other hand, talked a hard line and might even be capable of carrying out a large-scale military action to rescue the hostages. Was he all aggressive rhetoric or not? Rather than risk that uncertainty, Iran chose to reach an agreement with the Carter people.

Deadlines Reduce Your Opponent's Options

When you make an offer or counteroffer that contains a deadline for acceptance, you cut down your opponent's options significantly. How significantly depends upon the nearness of the deadline. Morgan's ten-minute deadline to Gates, for example, gave Gates almost no time to consider his options fully, which meant that he had in effect only one option—to settle. In contrast, had he not been pressured by a deadline, Gates could, and probably would, have taken his own sweet time to respond to Morgan's threat to start a competitive business, and he would have responded only after fully exploring all available options, including the sale of American Steel & Wire to others who might pay more than Morgan. Gates would have experienced virtually no anxiety. Moreover, he probably would have been delighted with the negotiating advantage that swung to him when Morgan (in this scenario) failed to force a decision within a definite time period.

With no deadline, your opponent has ample time to

explore other options. You then lose control and, thus, negotiating power. If your opponent does have available options, and the time to consider them, your power loss may be substantial. If your opponent does in fact choose another option, your power loss is total, since you have failed to reach your negotiating objectives.

Deadlines Give You Greater Flexibility

By setting deadlines, you are in a stronger position to formulate your plans effectively. Deadlines increase your control and your negotiating power.

For example, suppose you were negotiating the sale of a business with several prospective buyers. You receive a firm offer from the buyer you favor and anticipate offers from the others. In this position, you would invite chaos were you to make a counteroffer to that firm offer without including an acceptance deadline. Imposing a deadline would also dodge a potential legal hazard because most state laws allow "a reasonable time" for acceptance of offers and counteroffers when no deadline has been set. It would be unwise to let a vague "reasonable time" provision determine the fate of your negotiation when a definite deadline could be used to your advantage. Therefore, to keep control of the negotiation, and to keep the ball rolling with the party you prefer, you should be sure to incorporate a deadline for acceptance into your counteroffer.

Knowing the time in which your opponent must respond makes it easier for you to plan an appropriate course of action for either an acceptance or rejection. You are more in a position to guide the flow of the negotiation. Suppose you attach a ten-day deadline of acceptance to your counteroffer to the favored buyer. You can then begin planning immediately the counteroffers (if any) you intend to make to other prospective purchasers should your favored buyer respond negatively within that ten-day period. Assume that buyer makes a counteroffer to yours and gives you ten days in which to reply. Since you have already preplanned your strategy to include that possibility, you can decide your next course of action *immediately* and take full advantage of the ten days. You might, for instance, frame a counteroffer to another interested purchaser, including a deadline shorter than ten days for that individual's response. Hence, you can be considering a counteroffer made to you while another buyer is considering one of yours, all within the same time period. In this manner, you define and control the course of the negotiations. You achieve greater flexibility through deadlines, with a consequent greater chance of success.

SETTING THE DEADLINE PERIOD

Normally, the shorter the deadline period *that can be justified,* the greater the impact the deadline will have.

Morgan's deadline to Gates was only ten minutes, a very short time indeed. Under the circumstances, however, it was fully justified. Although Morgan had not taken an active role as the negotiations progressed—or failed to progress—throughout the day, Gates recognized that the absent power had been waiting during the entire period and with increasing impatience. Hence, when Morgan intervened, Gates could not feel offended by the short deadline because he knew Morgan had justification.

The Iranian hostage deadline was also very short. The Iranians could accept it, however, because it coincided with the lawful expiration of Christopher's authority to bargain. The deadline could, therefore, be fully justified.

Setting a deadline that is not justified is counterproductive because it creates resentment and anger. A resentful, angry opponent will become bold and, in most instances, react negatively to your proposals. To avoid this risk, you must carefully assess deadline length in light of the particular circumstances of each negotiation. Include in your calculations the personality, experience, and competence of your opponent. With all that in mind, set the shortest deadline that you can justify. Take pains to explain the basis for your deadline if you believe there is any chance your opponent will not understand your justification.

For illustrative purposes, consider the hypothetical case of John Smith, who owns a tool-and-die business and wants to sell out. Numerous people have expressed an interest, and three potential buyers (Mr. Olson, Mr. O'Hara, and Ms. Kleindienst) have submitted definite offers. All three offers are reasonably attractive but not sufficiently high for Smith to accept. Smith, in fact, prefers to sell to Kleindienst, because he feels she will be more apt to treat his employees, many of whom have been with the business a long time, with greater consideration. Smith does not wish to discourage Olson and O'Hara, however, because the competition will enhance his chance of getting a top price. Therefore, Smith submits a counteroffer to Kleindienst with a very short deadline for acceptance. He justifies the deadline by advising Kleindienst that other parties have a serious interest in the business and that he must respond to them in the near future. This approach is doubly effective. Smith has increased Kleindienst's anxiety by informing her, or reminding her, of the competition. In combination with the short deadline, this constitutes strong pressure on the buyer to accept the counteroffer.

AVOID IMPOSING DEADLINES ON YOURSELF

Frequently, negotiators will limit themselves with what might be termed *self-imposed* deadlines. They have the same impact as deadlines deliberately imposed on an opponent, only in reverse. As related earlier, I once benefited from an opponent's admission that he had a flight to catch at five o'clock in order to make an important meeting. He imposed upon himself a deadline. As the hour approached, his anxiety increased and his negotiating power waned.

Self-imposed deadlines are particularly common in real estate, especially in home sales. A case in point, I was negotiating the purchase of a large parcel of land that my client wanted as an investment. The seller lived on the land and was represented by a real estate broker. At one of our meetings, the broker casually mentioned that the seller was anxious to move into a new home, the construction of which was nearly complete, and needed the cash from this sale. That disclosure, of course, was a self-imposed deadline that substantially reduced the seller's negotiating power and materially increased mine. I now knew the seller would accept any reasonable purchase offer rather than hold out for the maximum price. Time was at a premium and it was on my side.

One of the most extraordinary self-imposed deadlines I have encountered occurred quite casually. I was waiting in the lobby of my opponent's office, chatting with his secretary. I complimented her on her nice suntan. She told me she had just come back from a vacation and that her boss, my opponent in the upcoming negotiation, was going to leave for a few days on his own vacation and hoped to get some sun himself. He was very tired and overworked, she continued, and he was greatly looking forward to getting away and just vegetating. That innocent conversation was a self-imposed deadline. I discovered that my tired opponent would be very receptive to settling our business before his scheduled vacation so that he could have peace of mind while soaking up the sun.

Often we face personal, or even professional, deadlines that cannot be altered and that have nothing to do with the matters under negotiation. The executive's five-o'clock flight, the property seller's new-home plans, and the boss's upcoming vacation were all legitimate parts of the lives of those individuals, but they would not necessarily have had a large impact on their respective negotiations had they remained private. The burden is on us as negotiators not to disclose information that can be converted into deadlines that will limit our flexibility and hinder our success. We want to impose deadlines on our opponents, not on ourselves.

As always, however, there can be exceptions. These may not have strategic validity. It is a question, really, of negotiating ethics.

Deliberately Set, Self-Imposed Deadlines

Not all self-imposed deadlines are the result of carelessness or accidents. At times, negotiators set deadlines for themselves *deliberately* for what can only be called selfish reasons. They find completing the negotiation is more important than obtaining the client's objectives. Once again, the real estate industry provides the illustrative cases.

Brokers usually work strictly on a commission basis. If they don't sell property, they don't earn any money. The great pressure to sell often results in brokers making untimely and unwarranted disclosures, some of which are self-imposed deadlines, to prospective buyers even though the brokers are legally representing the sellers. A broker might, for example, purposefully tip off the buyer that the seller needs the money from the sale to pay off a debt, take a trip, or meet any of a variety of pressing needs. The broker's design is to alert the buyer that the seller will be inclined to listen to any reasonable offer. Unless more than one buyer is interested in the property, the broker's disclosures have tipped the balance of negotiating power in favor of the buyer.

Be Alert, Even in Casual Conversations

Not only must you watch the disclosures you make during negotiations, you must be careful about inadvertent slips during casual conversations with your opponent, when normally your guard might be down. Experienced negotiators are aware that useful information can be harvested at these times. In fact, during casual meetings, one or both of the parties may deliberately try to guide the conversation towards potentially revealing topics.

Questions like, "Have you been traveling a lot?" or even, "Staying busy?" may appear innocent enough but could be asked with the purpose of eliciting responses that would indicate travel or other business timetables sufficiently pressing to constitute a hidden deadline. (Remember the executive with the essential five-o'clock flight and the boss who yearned for his vacation.) You must, therefore, consider *any* contact with your opponent at *any* time to be part of the actual negotiation. Remaining alert even during casual conversations will help eliminate those disclosures that could turn out to be costly self-imposed deadlines.

DEADLINE EXTENSIONS

The back edge of the double-edged sword of deadline setting usually does its cutting in the area of deadline extensions. Deadline extensions must be granted with great care and only when circumstances clearly warrant. The reason is obvious. If you extend a deadline without sufficient cause, your opponent will quite rightly conclude that you were bluffing. Your credibility will suffer irreparable harm, you will lose a tremendous amount of negotiating power, and your chances for success will decline precipitously.

It is best to grant extensions only out of necessity. I am reminded of a story about the tough cowhand who rode into a small Arizona town. Immediately planting himself in the local saloon, he soon began drinking whiskey by the bottle. The drunker he got, the meaner he got and took to wildly shooting up the place. No one dared stop him until a mild-mannered salesman sauntered into the saloon. He looked the situation over, walked up to the wild cowhand, and declared: "I'll give you five minutes to get out of town." To everyone's complete astonishment, the cowhand blinked a couple of times, dropped his gun into his holster, wobbled out to his horse, and rode away. A man in the disbelieving crowd finally shock himself out of his stupor and asked the salesman: "What would you have done if he hadn't left when the five minutes was up?" Without hesitation, the salesman replied: "I'd have extended the deadline."

In the Morgan-Gates confrontation described earlier, what would have happened had Morgan extended his ten-minute deadline to Gates? Gates believed that the competitive threat Morgan used to back up the deadline was serious. But would he have if Morgan had granted him a little more time to think things over? We'll never know for sure, of course, but one might speculate that the negotiating power Morgan gained by imposing a short deadline coupled with a competitive threat might have been substantially lessened had the deadline been lengthened.

When Should Deadlines Be Extended?

Deadline extensions should be granted only when newly discovered facts or circumstances warrant. If you have set a deadline, then before you allow an extension, you must be certain that any new information or situation *materially* alters the condition that justified the original deadline. Your opponent will be assessing the situation as well. If you extend the deadline without justification, you will have committed a serious strategic error that could reduce your negotiating power significantly.

Suppose the newly discovered facts or circumstances are not strong enough to really warrant a change of the deadline but are sufficient to merit serious consideration. For this borderline case, I have found that the best policy is to extend the deadline for only a short period. This approach sends a message to your opponent that you intend to stand by your deadline, but in order to be fair, you will allow a little flexibility. Rarely is any negotiating power lost, because the short extension is justified. Moreover, by communicating a desire for fairness, you have helped forge a bond of trust with the other negotiating party.

I want to stress that *justification* is the key to extending a deadline, as surely as it was for setting the deadline in the first place. If you can find no reasonable justification for extension, then you must adhere to the deadline. It is incumbent upon you to be absolutely certain that you are fully prepared to stand behind your set deadlines even if your offer or counteroffer is rejected. In this stance, you may emulate J. P. Morgan, who was certainly ready to start a competing business in the event Gates failed to accept his acquisition offer before the ten-minute deadline. Gates knew that Morgan was a man of his word, not a bluffer. You also want your negotiating opponents to know you are a person whose word can be trusted.

HANDLING DEADLINES IMPOSED BY YOUR OPPONENT

When your opponent gives you a deadline, you can respond in a number of ways. The most obvious response is to disregard the deadline. This approach, however, usually stalls the negotiation or kills it completely. That generally is not in your best interests. Two other more benign response options deserve consideration.

Respond within the Deadline

The primary problem with complying within a deadline is that you may experience considerable anxiety. And that raises the more substantial problem of shifting negotiating power to your opponent. That's precisely what happened to Gates when he faced a ten-minute deadline from Morgan. Similarly, the Iranians experienced the urgent need to work out a settlement for release of the American hostages with Carter's negotiators before the Carter administration relinquished its authority to deal.

Seek an Extension

Seeking an extension to your opponent's imposed deadline is an excellent approach. Gates should have appealed to Morgan's sense of fairness by pointing out that selling American Steel & Wire was both a substantial financial and emotional decision because of his attachment to the company. Chances are that Morgan, as a reasonable man, would have granted Gates an extension, perhaps as long as a week or two. Consider Morgan's private reaction after Gates caved in to his demands. It is reported that Morgan left the meeting site "as happy as a boy going home from a football game."[*]

True, the Iranians could not have gotten a deadline extension because, as much as he may have wanted to, Carter could not extend his stay in office. Nevertheless, the deadline was really in effect after the November election, essentially for two months. Christopher was merely reminding the Iranians of what they already should have known. Cleverly, he woke them up with 18 hours to go and quickly cut a deal for the safe release of the hostages.

In the final analysis, seeking deadline extensions is a sound negotiating strategy, especially when your opponent's imposed deadline is short. When your opponent grants a deadline extension, a portion of negotiating control shifts to you, and your negotiating power is enhanced by a corresponding amount. Therefore, you should seek a deadline extension whenever feasible and justifiable. As always, your strategic goal is to increase your control and power in order to reach your negotiating objectives.

---

[*]Frederick Lewis Allen, *The Great Pierpont Morgan* (New York: Harper & Brothers, 1949), 177.

CHAPTER 9

Determination, Persistence, and Mulish Stubbornness

Winners Never Quit, Quitters Never Win

The habit of persistence is the habit of victory.

Herbert Kaufman

Fix the goals you wish to gain, then go at it heart and brain.

Waterman

To him (or her) that is determined, it remains only to act.

Italian proverb

The human mind can achieve spectacular results through persistence, or, as some might say, stubbornness of purpose. This truth is vividly illustrated by the accomplishments of the great, the rich, and the notorious.

THE SUCCESS OF THE STUBBORN

J. Paul Getty, the late billionaire once reputed to be the richest person in America, attributed his great success to the qualities of "determination, persistence, and mulish stubbornness."*

Persistence is a common thread sewn through most success stories. Marshall Field, founder of the famous chain of department stores that bears his name, was once asked what he considered to have been essential to his career achievements. Without hesitation, he replied: "Perseverance."† That quality was tested when Field's home city of Chicago was almost entirely destroyed by fire in 1871. Even as the city smoldered, Field declared publicly that he would rebuild and that his new store would be bigger and better. He did and it was. Eventually, Field persevered to amass one of the largest personal fortunes of his time.

The story of another great commercial empire—McDonald's, America's largest restaurant chain—began a century later when its founder, Ray Kroc, was 52 years old. At that time, Kroc was suffering from diabetes and incipient arthritis and had lost part of his gall bladder and most of his thyroid gland. In the course of building McDonald's, Kroc encountered many roadblocks that would have stopped most people. For example, his

---

*Russell Miller, *The House of Getty* (New York: Henry Holt and Company, 1985), 123.
†*Forbes*, August 1, 1971, 62.

agreement with the McDonald brothers, the owners of the original California store, required that he follow their plan down to the last detail; any changes had to be in writing, signed by both brothers, and delivered to Kroc by registered mail. That special provision was to cause Kroc a lot of trouble.

Kroc lived in Illinois and wanted to open his first restaurant in Des Plains, Illinois. The Midwest has a season foreign to California: winter. The Des Plains restaurant required a basement to house the furnace; the McDonald brothers refused to give Kroc the necessary written approval. Two different lawyers quit while representing Kroc's negotiations with the recalcitrant Californians, advising Kroc that he was crazy to continue under those restrictions. Undeterred, Kroc plunged ahead, because nothing was going to stop him from building McDonald's into the great company he envisioned. As you are no doubt aware, today all McDonald's in the northern climes have heat.

It is not only business giants whose personality inspires study. Political leaders also have their fascination. For instance, many students of politics and human nature have been intrigued as to how Adolf Hitler was able to gain power and create a regime that was responsible for such monstrous and barbaric acts against humanity. During the Second World War, the allies had a more immediate and pragmatic purpose for understanding the German dictator. In 1943, a secret psychological report was written for William J. Donovan, head of the Office of Strategic Services (OSS), then America's basic intelligence agency. The report drew some conclusions concerning Hitler's outstanding talents and capacities:

> He has the "never-say-die" spirit. After some of his severest set-backs he has been able to get his immediate associates together and begin making plans for a "comeback." Events that would crush

most individuals, at least temporarily, seem to act as stimulants to greater efforts in Hitler.*

I do not mean to equate the contributions of Hitler to those of Getty, Field, and Kroc. My point is to portray the power of persistence, to show how people can overcome obstacles to achieve what no one would have thought possible.

PERSISTENCE PAYS

Persistence is a state of mind, and negotiation is mind versus mind. Hence, the same unbending persistence that propels goal-oriented business and political leaders also drives successful negotiators. In most negotiations, it matters little *at what point* your opponent says "yes" to your negotiating position, as long as he or she finally does say "yes." Therefore, you need only remain tenacious, and maintain a certain flexibility, to reach your objectives.

In Small Negotiations

Persistence paid off when I represented a client who was determined to have a motel constructed on the property adjoining his business. We approached a number of motel chains, lined up a suitable one, and offered top price to the owners of the property next to my client's business. Progress was being made until suddenly the property owners' interest in selling changed. Instead of selling to the motel chain what was only a portion of a larger

---

*Walter C. Langer, *The Mind of Adolf Hitler: The Secret Wartime Report* (New York: Basic Books, 1972), 75.

parcel, the owners decided they wanted to sell all the land. We came back with the proposal that my *client* would purchase the entire parcel from the owners and would then sell the necessary portion to the motel chain. The proposal included for the owners a profit-sharing arrangement on the net proceeds when my client was able to resell.

Negotiations progressed, and just when it appeared that an agreement would be finalized, the property owners changed their minds again. So we came up with a third proposal. Why not lease only the land desired by the motel chain for a designated number of years suitable to all parties, with an option to buy granted to the motel chain at the expiration of the term of the ground lease? Both the property owners and the motel chain liked this arrangement. The owners would receive rent for a known number of years and a sizable sum when the lease expired if the land was purchased. The motel chain would avoid a large cash outlay, incurring instead significantly smaller ground-lease payments that would be fully tax deductible as a business expense, thus increasing its net income.

My client, too, was happy because he got what he wanted. Persistence was the key that unlocked the door to making the deal.

And Large Negotiations, Too

In another instance, a claim of $9,925,894.93 was made against my clients. The issues were numerous and complex, as they generally are when so much money is involved. I knew my two opponents would be extremely well prepared. I also knew the negotiations would entail a number of sessions and follow a circuitous path to the eventual agreement, again because so much money was involved. I was certain persistence would play a pivotal role in determining the final outcome.

My primary objective was to reduce the $9,925,894.93 to 15 percent of that amount, or approximately $1,475,000. It was a tough goal. I set it because experience had taught me that loftier goals bring forth greater efforts. Naturally, I had first ascertained through a scrutiny of the facts and applicable law that my objective was reachable.

The ensuing negotiations were indeed tough, hard-hitting, and aggressive, and, as I had anticipated, spread over several sessions. Many times I had to find a way around a seeming impasse with a new approach or a variation on an old one. The $9.9+ million began to melt away. Still, discussions continued until my opponents agreed to a figure of $1,533,000, only slightly more than my primary objective.

At this juncture, my clients were happy and receptive to settling. I recommended, however, that we seek a further reduction. I reasoned that the negotiating momentum was with us and should be exploited to the fullest. My clients agreed to continue.

By now, I could sense my opponents cringing when they heard my voice on the telephone asking for another personal meeting. On one occasion, they suggested we discuss the matter over the phone. I tactfully declined. Since I had made excellent progress in face-to-face negotiations, I wanted to maintain the advantage of that medium. I also knew that people tend to be tougher, bolder, and less prone to compromise when they don't have to look their opponent (in this case, me) in the eye. This tendency particularly holds true when the negotiator has already made substantial concessions, as was the case here. No, I wasn't going to let them get away with telephone negotiations.

The next negotiating session was especially tough. That was to be expected because my opponents had already made substantial concessions and had agreed to continue negotiating only with reluctance. The best approach in these situations is to hammer away on the merits of your case, the facts, the law, or anything that supports your position. In this way, you force your opponents to concentrate on the subject matter of the negotiation and forget their displeasure with the results and with having to continue to meet.

My persistence paid off. I was able to reduce the final amount awarded to $1,066,207.80, less than 11 percent of the original figure sought.

WHAT PERSISTENCE REALLY MEANS

Persistence is an energizing force for the mind. It is a catalyst for action. Persistence is what drives you to find new ways to continue a stalled negotiation. That's nice, you say. But what does persistence really mean?

Persistence Is Not . . .

There are many ways to be persistent. Kids often get their way by relentlessly begging until the parent gives in. Many street peddlers use that same approach, aided by a mixture of hassling, harassing, and, on occasion, even bullying to make a sale. My old infantry sergeant was an expert at intimidation. He had a deep, always angry voice, developed over 20 years of barking out commands, and a penetrating stare that went through you like a gale wind through leafless trees. He punctuated his orders by slamming his helmet to the ground or, more likely, on to the hood of a jeep, leaving a sizable dent in the unfortunate vehicle—and in our minds.

Begging, hassling, harassing, bullying, and intimidating are, in fact, everyday occurrences in the business and professional world. For some people, that constitutes the normal way of communicating, and getting, what they want. They use economic and legal threats to intimidate others. Often these tactics work against those in a weaker position who are literally forced to submit. But the benefits are only short term. The intimidated are frequently resentful and willing to wait for the opportunity to get revenge. Sooner or later that opportunity comes.

In negotiation, these tactics are counterproductive because they frequently make an opponent angry. As mentioned earlier, anger polarizes the negotiating parties and stifles negotiating progress. All to often, I've encountered opponents who have resorted to intimidating tactics in an attempt to achieve their objectives. The approach only makes them vulnerable. Every time they beg, hassle, harass, or bully, I counter with a request that they explain factually and/or legally why I should concur with their position. As long as they continue their improper tactics, I continue to counter with my request, until they discuss the issues in a rational and reasonable manner. I then have the opportunity to convince them to agree with my position.

Persistence is *not* an attempt at attrition through extended irritation. That is for children or for adults with arrested development.

Persistence Is . . .

Persistence is an attitude of determination. When you reach an impasse in discussions, when progress has come to a virtual halt, the persistent person creates new, fresh approaches; comes up with new supporting facts, law, or arguments; finds a new insight into the problem that is hampering the negotiations. In the large litigation case cited previously, this sort of persistence enabled me to find ways to reduce the original $9.9+ million to just over

$1 million. My opponents were too experienced to let anyone beg, hassle, harass, or bully them into a settlement. My persistence and ingenuity wore at them successfully; obnoxious behavior would not have succeeded.

WHEN YOU HAVE EXHAUSTED YOUR POSITIONS

What do you do when you have spent virtually all your resources, exhausted all available arguments, and still haven't attained your negotiating objectives? Where do the resources come from to break through the impasse and win more concessions? You investigate the best source: your opponent.

Your opponent may disclose a fact, a point of law, or some information that either by itself or in combination with information you already possess can provide the raw material for a new approach. The dynamics of two people freely discussing all aspects of an issue invariably results in exchanges that will broaden the knowledge and strengthen the grasp of each party of that issue. Thus, the sharp negotiator who possesses a good, analytical mind will create something positive from the dynamic energy inherent in the give and take of negotiations. An opportunistic negotiator is able to do this on the spot in the middle of discussions, take advantage of the element of surprise, and place the opponent on the defensive.

I consider my opponents fertile sources of helpful information, which I openly seek at virtually every negotiation of importance and use, if possible, right at those opportune moments.

IF AT FIRST YOU DON'T SUCCEED, KEEP TRYING

When on the topic of persistence, I invariably think of the story of the gold prospector who discovered a mine and worked it until the vein of gold was played out. He continued to drill, however, searching for that vein of gold, but always without success. Finally, he quit and sold out to a junk dealer. The junk dealer hired an engineer, who calculated that the vein would be found just three feet from the spot where the miner had stopped drilling. The gold was, in fact, where predicted, and the junk dealer made millions.*

Remember That "Three Feet"

When I reach a negotiating impasse, I always remind myself of that vein of gold that was just three feet away. The recollection spurs on my persistent nature. In fact, I frequently keep discussions going simply to be continually exposed to my opponent in the hope of learning something that will spark an idea that will give us a breakthrough. Interestingly enough, the person on the other side of the negotiating table is frequently motivated to keep talking by the same hope that something will happen, although neither one wants to be the one to make the revealing disclosure.

---

*Napolean Hill, *Think and Grow Rich* (New York: Hawthorne Books, 1965), 20, 21.

CHAPTER 10

Making Sure the Door Is Closed and Locked

The Right Ways to Close a Negotiation

What'er the course, the end is the renown.

Shakespeare

Closing is one of the most critical phases of negotiation. Some negotiators are quite skillful in the negotiating art, yet fail miserably at the closing, often with disastrous consequences. Lacking the ability to bring down the curtain successfully, they are, thus, just good talkers, not truly good negotiators.

FOUR LITTLE WORDS

I negotiated against a great talker very early in my career. I was in my late 20s, and he was in his middle 60s. He advocated his position forcefully, yet smoothly, with soft, carefully chosen words that made the point but didn't offend. I sat there marveling at his logic, his persuasiveness, his evenness. His deep, rich voice was reassuring and comforting. As the negotiation ran on, I began looking forward to each session as an opportunity to enjoy his performance and learn from his expertise. Soon, he had me convinced of the merits of his position. I was hooked, and all he had to do was reel me in. He could have done so with four little words: "Then it is agreed." He never did. He committed, instead, one of the most common and cardinal sins of closing. He suggested that I "think it over."

Any experienced fisherman will tell you that when you have the lake record on your hook, you reel it in and put in your net. You don't fight the fish up to the boat and then invite it to ponder whether it wants to be caught. Few game fish are so accommodating. Even very young and impressionable negotiators seldom give up when given the option to "think it over."

THE MOST CRITICAL CLOSING ELEMENT: TIMING

In the Bible we are taught that: "To everything there is a season, and a time for every matter under heaven."* Shakespeare put it differently, if no less eloquently, in *Julius Caesar:*

> There is a tide in the affairs of men
> Which, taken at the flood, leads on to fortune;
> Omitted, all the voyage of their life
> Is bound in shallows and in miseries.†

Timing is the most critical element in closing. Unintentionally, involuntarily, unwittingly, or even inadvertently losing it is bad enough, and the negotiator will, of course, have to suffer the resulting misfortune. Intentionally losing one's timing, however, is quite something else. Suggesting that I "think it over" when I was ready to be landed let me off the hook. I could return to my office, safe from the very persuasive talents of my opponent, and ponder the negotiation objectively—which, of course, I did. When next we met, I raised a number of objections to the great talker's position that enabled me to win material concessions.

WHEN IS THE RIGHT TIME TO CLOSE?

Each negotiation is unique. Even if the parties happen to have met before across the table under similar circumstances, the issues on the next occasion will be different and discussed in a new context. The critical time to close is special to each negotiation. Knowing precisely when to close is a subjective, almost instinctive, talent that can be sharpened with experience and a growing understanding of human nature.

You must always be asking yourself whether your

---

*Ecclesiastes 3:1.
†William Shakespeare, *Julius Caesar*, Act IV, Scene 3.

opponent is ready to say "yes" to your position. When you decide it is time, then the moment to close has arrived. That time may occur at virtually any point in the negotiation, including the very beginning when discussions have barely gotten under way. Perhaps your opponent is the decisive type (most are not) who knows precisely what he or she wants and doesn't appreciate wasting time. These situations most often occur when price is the primary matter to be negotiated. Your opponent knows exactly what price is acceptable, and, if that figure is mutually agreed upon at the onset of negotiations, the matter can quickly be brought to a close. Just recently, I participated in such a situation as representative of the seller of a piece of property. The buyer, a large corporation, made a top offer at the onset, which my client quickly accepted. With only preliminary matters to be cleared up, the negotiation didn't take more than five minutes.

The time to close may occur at what you might be anticipating as the middle of the negotiation. In many negotiations, particularly when the person across the table represents a large corporation and must answer to higher powers, your opponent may want to build a complete file for a formal report and as personal security should someone later check into the transaction. You may have to go through a process of "educating" your opponent on the merits of your position before a comfort zone is reached and you can close. You might arrive at that point quite suddenly, in the midst of your "re-explanation," and so must be alert to the chance of finalizing, so to speak, in the middle.

The time to close may not come until the discussion has run its course, when both parties are completely exhausted, having advanced every possible position and counterposition. Closure most commonly comes "at the end" when the negotiation involves controversy, as in lawsuits and other similar disputes. The parties slug it out until both eventually and inevitably decide it's time to close. Unfortunately some lawyers habitually close at the very end of the negotiation (often on the courthouse steps) to run up their fees. Most attorneys, however, seek to close as quickly and judiciously as possible.

The burden is on the negotiator to determine when the critical time has arrived and to take immediate steps to close. Failure to seize the moment can be extremely costly.

STAY ALERT FOR CLUES

Searching for signs that your opponent is ready to say "yes" means paying careful attention to *what* is said and *how* it is said. You listen attentively to your opponent's words and tone of voice and watch attentively your opponent's body language. Normally, words, tone, and body language must be considered together to determine accurately your opponent's true state of mind.

Your Opponent's Language

Language consists of both written and spoken words. Letters, memos, and even hastily jotted notes will all reflect your opponent's attitude and state of mind. For example, written and spoken words that are positive, agreeable, and upbeat toward your positions are an excellent indication that your opponent may be ready to say "yes." Therefore, hearing or reading the following constitutes an encouraging sign: *yes, uh-huh, I agree, sounds fine to me, okay, good*, and *sure*. On the other hand, you don't want to encounter: *no, can't, won't, not clear* (your position), *hardly*, and *not*.

And then, of course, there are shades of gray. Neutral words such as *maybe, possibly, perhaps*, and *might* tend to indicate that your opponent is undecided and that you'll have to work a little harder before attempting to close. Suppose your opponent says that what you are advocating *possibly* has merit. You can read that as a neutral stance and continue to negotiate. If you can change *possibly* to *certainly* or elicit *sounds fine to me* or even *uh-huh*, then the time may be ripe to close. If, on the other hand, your opponent says what you are advancing is *not clear* or *hardly* a good position, you know you still have a long way to go to get to "yes."

Your Opponent's Tone of Voice

Aside from the meaning of the actual words themselves, does your opponent *sound* strong, decisive, firm, even perhaps a little arrogant? Then your opponent is probably not ready to say "yes." If the voice sounds mild, cooperative, submissive, or even neutral, then your opponent may be ripe to utter "yes."

Look for Consistency

The words your opponent speaks should be consistent with the tone in which they are spoken; that is, positive language should be reinforced by a positive tone. If not, you should not usually seek to close negotiations at that point. Conversely, you might hear a positive tone with negative language. In fact, that combination is not unlikely, since skilled negotiators are frequently skilled actors and perfectly capable of sounding more encouraging than their actual words warrant. If the language is either negative or neutral but the tone is positive, you can correctly conclude that the time is not yet ripe to attempt to close the negotiation.

Body Language

We tell others all about ourselves by the way we look, the way we move, and by the postures we assume. Indeed, the language of our body is often more revealing than our words and tone of voice, because body appearance, movements, and positions are often subconscious, or natural, rather than consciously controlled to deceive. Even skilled negotiators who are also skilled actors cannot consistently manipulate body language as readily as speech. While they are concentrating on controlling what they are saying and how to say it, their mind is communicating to their body their true mental state. The voice may be articulating a firm "no," but the body may be positioned to say "yes."

Here are some elemental messages the body communicates. A body in strenuous motion, say jogging, informs us that the owner has become health conscious, either voluntarily or out of illness-inspired necessity. A slim and trim jogger communicates a diet consciousness as well. The message of an obese person tells the opposite story of a sedentary lifestyle embellished by overeating. A neatly dressed, precisely groomed person reveals a perfectionist, one who functions best when everything is orderly and in its right place.

Three Not-Always-Little "Words"

The three aspects of human anatomy—appearance, movement, and posture—are the three "words" that constitute body language. Taken in sum, they reveal more to a person who can read them than spoken and written words. Consider the following unlikely combination for illustrative purposes: your opponent is telling you in a sweet, cooperative tone that your positions are sound and fully agreeable, but at the same time is shaking a clenched fist in your face. I think it is safe to conclude that the body language reflects your opponent's true state of mind more accurately than speech and tone of voice.

It is obviously worthwhile to train your powers of observation to read body language. Your primary interest in reading body language is to ascertain whether your opponent's appearance, movement, or posture is negative. If so, your opponent is not likely to say "yes," and you would be unwise to attempt to close negotiations. On the other hand, if you can detect no negative body signals, then you can proceed on your assumption that your opponent's positive speech and tone truly reflect a desire to close. Note, however, that negative body language will normally override positive spoken or written words and tone. Recall that body language is more difficult to control and, therefore, more likely to represent an honest communication of state of mind.

Accordingly, you must learn what constitutes negative body language. Negotiators who fail to acquire this ability will be in for a rude awakening when their attempt to close is rebuffed by an opponent who "sounded" ready. That surprise can be a confidence-shaking experience, especially for those who consider themselves skilled in the art of negotiation.

Examples of Common Negative Body Language

No matter how simple or complex the negotiation, you are very apt to see someone express negative feelings/attitudes with their body positions in one or several of the following ways. You may be doing them yourself and, thus, communicating unconsciously valuable information to your opponent.

1. *Arms folded across the chest.* This is a classic defensive posture. It usually means the person either opposes or disbelieves what he or she is hearing.

2. *Body turned sideways with an arm draped over the back of the chair and legs crossed.* This position is often combined with the person leaning away from the negotiator as if repelled by what he or she is advocating. The crossed legs and turned torso are shielding gestures; the leaning away suggests an attempt to distance one's self from the other. The position should, thus, not be confused with a relaxation pose.

3. *Body turned sideways and leaning away.* This is a less emphatic variation of the position above, but without the draped arm. It is frequently combined with the corners of the mouth turning down. It communicates repulsion (leaning away) and is very negative (turned torso, turned down mouth) toward the position being advocated.

4. *Chin resting in the palm of the hand, with arm held tightly against the body and head tilted slightly away.* This posture indicates opposition or disbelief. The tighter the chin-rest arm is against the body, the more pronounced is the person's desire to be shielded or protected from the position being advocated.

5. *Eyes revolving upwards.* The eyes move gradually and often stop temporarily, while looking directly upwards. This eye action normally conveys disbelief.

6. *Hand held in front of the person's own face.* Sometimes this face-shielding action of the hand is combined with rubbing the nose. The hand is a physical manifestation of a psychological need for a barrier to ward off the advocated position. This

posture is frequently exhibited by inexperienced negotiators who lack confidence in their ability to cope. When you encounter this gesture, expect to spend time and patience on setting the person's mind at ease. When the hand moves and stays away from your opponent's face, you know you have made some progress.

7. *Corners of the mouth turned downward.* This common expression is a clear indication that the person is negative toward what is being advocated.

Each of these negative body expressions may appear separately, or they may follow one another in succession. For example, your opponent might begin by turning the corners of his mouth downward, then slowly turning away from you, crossing his legs, draping an arm over the back of the chair, and leaning away until he has adopted a fixed, clearly negative position. Or, you may have an opponent turn to the side and lean away from you, then slowly revolve her eyes upward. She might shift from one negative position to another, perhaps beginning with the corners of her mouth turned downward, then relax her mouth to a normal position but fold her arms tightly across her chest.

A Note of Caution

Not every movement tells a story. We all shift our position when required to sit in one place for an extended time, as is frequently the case in negotiations. Be aware, therefore, that an opponent's change in position may be an attempt to get comfortable rather than a signal of rejection. However, by shifting from one negative posture to another, your opponent is clearly indicating that he or she is not receptive to what you are advocating. Holding a negative position for an extended period, perhaps five minutes or more, is another indicator of disapproval. As you gain experience, you will more easily distinguish between body relaxation movements and body language that reveals a mental state.

THE KEY ROLE OF QUESTIONS

Suppose you have expended your best efforts to place your opponent in a positive mental state conducive to closing the negotiation successfully. But your opponent's words, tone of voice, and body language all reflect negative feelings. Normally, you do not attempt to close, because if your attempt is rejected, your opponent will have a tendency to dig in and resist closing until you make concessions. The burden is on you to find a way to convert your opponent's negativism. An excellent approach is to ask questions.

To illustrate, I was negotiating with a broker for the acquisition of a parcel of real estate. The broker was anxious to consummate the transaction, but when it came time to close, his tone of voice was hesitant, even though his spoken and body languages were positive. Rather than proceed, I decided to clear up the reason for his apparent reluctance.

"I think we're both ready to put the finishing touches on this," I said, "but your tone seems somewhat hesitant. Is there something troubling you?"

Notice I didn't say, "What's troubling you?" That's too definite and tends to magnify any problems the individual may be experiencing. By framing my question with "Is there" rather than "What's," I probed into my opponent's negativism in a milder way that facilitated further negotiation.

Notice also that my purposely mild question still cut to the heart of the matter: the reason for the broker's negative tone of voice. When the negotiation is nearly set to close and you perceive an obstacle, do not hesitate to break through that barrier as quickly and effectively as possible. You may be particularly assertive when you have a good relationship with the other party, as I did in this instance, because your opponent is not apt to become defensive nor likely to seize your question as an opportunity to seek more concessions. When a degree of animosity exists between you, however, you will have to be more cautious.

By this time I had, of course, funneled the negotiation down to a very tiny outlet, so asking evasive or too-general questions would have run an unnecessary risk of widening the funnel and losing control of the negotiation. Hence, I proceeded tactfully to the heart of the matter and was rewarded by the broker's visible relief. He said the attorney representing his client was constantly constructing roadblocks out of trivia and thrusting them into his path (an example of why attorneys have, unfortunately, developed a reputation as deal killers). As a result, the broker needed certain minor adjustments to pacify the attorney. The adjustments were quickly granted, and the negotiation was closed.

ONCE THE DOOR IS CLOSED, LOCK IT

Take great care to be certain that closed negotiations remain that way. This means that all post-closing contacts between you and your opponent are relegated to winding up the matter. Tactfully and firmly cut off any attempts by your opponent to delve into nonclosing matters. Usually a comment like "That's already been agreed to," or similar language, will get discussions back on track.

A particularly critical period is immediately after the negotiation has been closed and the parties must spend time together, perhaps sharing a taxi or having dinner.

Don't let the conversation drift back to the negotiation. It's too risky. Your opponents might have been entertaining third or fourth thoughts about their decisions and, therefore, might welcome an opportunity to open any facet of the negotiations. Self doubt, as related, seems to weigh heaviest on the inexperienced. Talk about family, sports, travel, anything that does not touch on the negotiations just completed. Keep that door shut tight.

CLOSING TECHNIQUES

Closing techniques are cues for the close; they are not devices for "winning" the negotiation. If your opponent is not ready to say "yes" to your position, employing a closing technique is valueless and could even be harmful. At the very least, your opponent will be puzzled by what you are doing and could easily resent it, considering your behavior presumptuous and, thus, building a degree of animosity toward you.

Think of the closing technique as the starter's pistol that sends the runners down the track at the beginning of the race. The race is really the culmination of weeks, months, even years of strenuous and disciplined effort. The runners are thoroughly trained and ready for action when they take their positions in the blocks—just as you have thoroughly completed the negotiation and prepared your opponent to say "yes" to your position. Use of the closing technique is the starter's "gunshot" that prompts your opponent to "spring into action" to close the negotiation and see the "race" to its conclusion.

The Prompting-Action Technique

As the name implies, you effectuate the close by calling upon your opponent to take some form of action. This technique is commonly used in sales and advertising. At the end of a super-car-sale commercial, for example, the speaker might encourage the audience to: "Come in now! The deal ends soon!"—an enticement that is designed to compel action.

In negotiation, this technique is applied when you place a document in front of your opponent and request a signature or when you prompt an affirmative oral response or even a nod of the head with the inviting phrase, "I'm sure you agree." Notice that was a statement, not a question. You ask questions only when you want to control your opponent's choice of answers. For instance: "Do you want our office to prepare the closing agreements (contracts, leases, and so forth) or does your office want to prepare them?" Your phrasing confines your opponent's response to matters related to the closing and avoids matters relevant to the subject of the negotiation. That's an important distinction. Remember, you don't want to give your opponent an opportunity to reopen any phase of the negotiation.

The Assumption Technique

Here you make certain assumptions that are, again, designed to institute closing. This technique doesn't prompt actions through suggestions or questions, it assumes the other party will agree. The statement "I'll call the bank and ask them to set up the escrow" is an example. It takes for granted your opponent will go along. You then proceed under that assumption to prompt your opponent toward a definite course of action, in this case, setting up the escrow.

Suppose instead of saying "I'll call the bank and ask them to set up the escrow," you ask, "Shall I call the bank and ask them to set up the escrow?" The second statement is obviously quite different from the first. The first statement assumes agreement; the second, a question, assumes nothing and *asks* your opponent's permission to effect the closing. It risks rewidening the funnel because your opponent could very well seize the opportunity to seek additional concessions before answering "yes."

The assumption technique should be practiced with care and tact. You do not want your opponents to believe they are being strong-armed into an agreement. You should be certain, as well, that your opponent in each case will be receptive to this approach, that is, to the assumption you are making.

The Summarizing Technique

This a highly effective technique and my personal favorite because it reassures the other party. You summarize the substance of the agreement to establish a clear understanding of the terms and conditions; in the process, you are using repetition to help cement the agreement even more firmly in your opponent's mind.

I very recently used this technique to close a particularly difficult negotiation that had extended over six months. It had been essentially a cat-and-mouse game. We would reach an agreement; then my opponent would renege and reopen negotiations. After several "false" closings, I became determined to finalize the business once and for all. I did so with the summarizing technique. By carefully summarizing the details of the agreement and getting my opponent to acknowledge each detail, I made it virtually impossible for him to again renege. He tried, but I brushed off his attempts by referring to my summarization that he had concurred with at that time. That's an advantage of the technique: it pins your opponent down.

Here is another example of how the summarizing

technique works. Assume you acquire a large tract of land for development. You want to remove a house from the land to make room for a road. The house is in good condition, and you prefer to sell it and have it moved rather than tear it down. You want to be certain that the mover has enough liability insurance to cover any accidents that may occur while transporting the house. You also want the mover to fill in the basement after the house is moved so no one will inadvertently stumble into the foundation hole, hurt themselves, and sue you. Finally, you want the mover to have the house off the land by a definite date so you can schedule construction of the development you have planned. Upon reaching an understanding on these matters with the mover, you can employ the summarizing technique as follows:

> You: Let's make sure everything is clear. The total cost of moving the house is $10,000. The house is to be moved by August 1st. The basement of the house is to be graded over completely. In addition, you will provide written evidence, satisfactory to me, that you have in force at least $500,000 of liability insurance that will cover me.
>
> MOVER: That's right.

By use of the summarizing technique, you have not only neatly tied up the substance of the agreement but also have obtained an affirmative, confirming response from the mover. You can see why this is such an effective closing technique and my favorite.

Appendix

A Negotiator's Checklist

The following list reproduces, more or less in the order they were covered, the main topics and subtopics of the book. Use it as a handy study guide before your next negotiation.

- Exploit your opponents's mental rigidity.
  - — Draw out their mental frame with questions.
  - — Derail their one-track minds.
  - — Use their predictability to gain an edge.
- Remain flexible.
  - — Prepare for each issue thoroughly.
  - — Have a general strategy, but avoid a preset formula.
  - — Expect the unexpected
- Identify the person who has final negotiating authority.
  - — Don't let them double team you.
  - — Just ask.
  - — Don't be fooled by title, age, or appearance.
  - — Be observant.
  - — Take few notes.
  - — Don't let your guard down.
  - — Watch for the reluctant authority.
- Reach the final authority through conduits.
- Apply the oblique approach.
- Assess the authority of the intermediary.
- Discover what your opponent fears.
- Recognize your own power.
  - — Employ the "power think time" technique.
- Use your power in a timely manner.

- Let your opponent know you have power.
- Don't waste your power by holding it in reserve.
- Use a variety of sensory stimulations for effective repetition.
- Don't lose sight of your primary base.
  - Set specific objectives on each issue.
  - Remain cool under pressure.
  - Avoid smoking and bad eating habits.
  - Take a break when you need one.
- Identify and use secondary bases.
- Don't lose sight of your secondary bases.
  - Avoid distractions.
  - Use the list-and-check system.
- Find new secondary bases during negotiations by asking questions.
- Equalize your opponent's every position.
  - Advance positions of equal or greater weight.
  - Demonstrate the weakness of your opponent's position.
  - Set aside your opponent's position.
  - Keep your opponent fully informed about relevant facts.
  - Show the irrelevance of your opponent's position.
- Equalize even far-out positions.
- Take advantage of your opponent's failure to equalize.
- Always seek to control the negotiations.
  - Try to meet on your home field.
  - Try to meet at your best time of day.
  - Try to determine the order of discussion.

— Scrutinize the documents your opponent will see.

— Avoid adding new elements.

— Avoid language that will anger your opponent.

• Practice funneling.

— Don't let new elements rewiden the funnel.

— Employ countertactics when needed.

— Make postnegotiation analysis a habit.

— Keep resolved issues closed.

• Let your opponent make the first offer.

• Explain the basis for any offer or counteroffer you make.

• Remember: each counteroffer is an entirely new offer.

• Use counteroffers to:

— facilitate the finalizing process, and

— exercise control.

• Avoid the polarization that comes from unwise ultimatums.

• Insert an *unless* into your ultimatums.

• Stay cool when your offer or counteroffer is rejected.

• Avoid lowballing and highballing.

• Be sure you understand your opponent's offers and counteroffers.

— Seek clarification if needed.

— Repeat the specifics of the terms and conditions.

• Respond calmly to lowball or highball offers.

• Set deadlines to:

— create anxiety in your opponent,

— reduce your opponent's options, and

— give yourself greater flexibility.

• Set deadlines for as short a time as you can justify.

- Be alert to your opponent's self-imposed deadlines.
- Avoid imposing deadlines on yourself.
- Grant deadline extensions only when new facts and/or circumstances warrant.
- Seek extensions when your opponent gives you a deadline.
- Be persistent in pursuit of your negotiating objectives.
  - Try different approaches.
  - Find new arguments.
  - Seek new information.
- Converse with your opponent to find new options.
- Remember: persistence is *not* begging, hassling, harassing, or bullying.
- Persistence is an attitude of determination.
- Never invite your opponent to "think the matter over."
- Always ask yourself if your opponent is ready to say "yes."
- Stay alert for clues that it is time to close.
  - Listen to your opponent's words.
  - Pay attention to your opponent's tone of voice.
  - Translate your opponent's body language.
  - Look for consistency between your opponent's speech, tone, and body language.
- Question your opponent carefully about negative signs.
- Use closing techniques when the time is right.
  - Call upon your opponent to take action.
  - Assume your opponent will agree.
  - Summarize the substance of the agreement.
- Don't let your opponent open closed negotiations.

Index